Cooking Ahead

COOKING AHEAD

BARBARA WORSLEY-GOUGH

with a foreword by
ANDRÉ SIMON

FABER AND FABER LIMITED
24 Russell Square
London

*First published in mcmlvii
by Faber and Faber Limited
24 Russell Square London W.C.1
Printed in Great Britain by
Latimer Trend & Co Ltd Plymouth
All rights reserved*

TX
717
.W93
1957

TO HENRY
WITH LOVE AND GREED

Contents

FOREWORD *by* André Simon	*page* 11
COOKING AHEAD—INTRODUCTION	13
NECESSARY STORES	18
BATTERIE DE CUISINE	20
SAUCES	25
SOUP	31
EGGS	42
FISH	48
PASTA	63
RICE	70
BIRDS	77
MEAT DISHES: BEEF	89
PORK	95
VEAL	98
MUTTON	104
VARIOUS HOT SUPPER DISHES	110
MOUSSES AND PÂTÉS	114
VEGETABLES	121
SALADS	132
PUDDINGS	137
MENUS FOR DINNER AND SUPPER	147

Foreword

Barbara Worsley-Gough could easily and most engagingly have written a cookery book on the 'those were the days' theme, but she has done nothing of the sort. On the contrary, she has resolutely turned her back on the days when there were servants and when everything that was best could so easily be yours. Looking ahead and realizing that conditions are very different today, and are likely to be even more different presently, she has written a book which gives the hostess of today and tomorrow sound advice on how to entertain her friends at home: how to give them original and good food, which will have been prepared before the evening of the party, so that it may be enjoyed by hostess and guests alike without constantly running from the dining-room to the kitchen—which is so embarrassing for the guests and far from pleasant for the hostess.

There are a great many cookery books published every year: some are good and others are not so good; Barbara Worsley-Gough's book has its place among the good ones, and as it certainly strikes an entirely new note it should have a very wide appeal.

ANDRÉ L. SIMON

Introduction

I wrote down the recipes in this book as I cooked, because it occurred to me that other people might be glad of a collection of recipes for food that can be cooked comfortably in advance of the parties at which it will be eaten.

I believe that cooking ahead is the solution of the problem of entertaining without any servants, but it makes nonsense of about three-quarters of the recipes in almost all cookery books. This book deals only with dishes that can be made well beforehand, good food that is concocted peacefully and attentively in the spare moments of Monday or Tuesday, for the dinner-party on Wednesday. Of course it means abandoning the traditional English roasts and grills, and a very good thing too. Most people eat these things several times a week all the year round, and when they go out to dinner, or give a dinner-party, they might just as well have something which is delicious in a different way.

Plain English cookery at its best is superb, but it needs constant skilled attention at every stage if it is to be really good. There are perhaps few better dinners than grilled sole, roast saddle of mutton with all its accompaniments, cherry pie, and grilled mushrooms on toast—but this regional feast is completely beyond the powers of the cook-hostess. If she feels obliged to produce a dinner like this for her guests, she would probably do better to engage a deputy hostess for the evening, and spend her time in solitary activity at the kitchen stove.

The truth is that English cookery is not, as a whole, suitable

Introduction

for the servantless household. It was evolved through centuries of modest prosperity in farmhouses and manors, where scullions were numerous and very cheap to employ, when it was usual for three or four women and girls to be kept busy all day in the kitchen and dairy and still-room producing the food for one household. With the disappearance of the scullions, and then of the trained and practical cook, the traditional dishes remained the staple diet of the country, but became plainer and plainer and duller and duller because nobody had time to make the sauces, and dress the vegetables, and stuff the fish, and beat the eggs and the cream, all of which once gave richness and variety to the splendid raw material of English food. Then a generation reared on this changed and limited English cookery began to speak contemptuously of 'greasy French food' and 'foreign kickshaws', and to demand food prepared in apocalyptic ruthlessness with the two elements of fire and water. Butter was used only to put on bread, never on vegetables; gravy became a pasty concoction of flour half-cooked in hot dripping; and sauce, something horrible in a bottle from the grocer's. It is a sad deterioration in the taste of the people who once liked its food seasoned with more than twenty varieties of pot-herbs, and coined the picturesome adage 'Fine words butter no parsnips'.

So the good old standard English dishes, and the bad new 'plain roast or boiled' ones have been eliminated when planning the menus in this book. I have included only what I cook for my own parties, and the range is necessarily limited by my own tastes, prejudices, and pocket. I can't afford salmon or game, I dislike hot puddings, and don't make ices because that disorganizes the contents of my old-fashioned refrigerator. I disapprove of the frying-pan, and am not fond of pastry. My kitchen is in the basement and there is no lift to the dining-room, and so I plan my dinners with a view to making only one trip to the kitchen during dinner, and having everything, except one hot course, prepared and left ready in the dining-room before the party begins. Soup can be put boiling-hot into a large thermos jug and the plates kept warm on a heater on the side-table. If the first course is a cold one, it is ready on the table. The cold pudding and its plates,

Introduction

the salad if there is one, the dessert-plates and the fruit are all put on the sideboard in readiness. Sometimes I ask my Mrs. Morning-Help to come back for an hour or so in the evening, and then I can have hot fish as well as a hot main course, and a pudding which may stay in the refrigerator until the last minute on a hot night, because she will bring it up when I ring. If you have a kitchen close to the dining-room it is easier to collect the next course rapidly, but I think it is important for the hostess not to break up the beautiful contentment of talking and eating more than once in the course of the evening, if it can be avoided.

Cooking ahead doesn't mean getting the worst of it over by tea-time on the day of the party. It means doing most of it the day before—or, if necessary, the day before that. If you have a refrigerator or a really cold larder, there is no virtue in devoting half a day to the cooking of one meal, when you can make the various dishes at any convenient time during the preceding day or two, and leave them ready to be reheated for the dinner-party. Most dishes of meat can be cooked forty-eight hours ahead, cold fish dishes and cold puddings (except those with cream in them) twenty-four hours ahead. Vegetables and salad should be bought (or gathered) fresh on the day that they will be eaten.

When I have a dinner-party, I finish off the cooking in the morning. The soup or the fish or other first course, is in the larder, the pudding in the refrigerator. I decant the wine, and put the silver, glasses, and cold plates on trays. At six o'clock I lay the table, arrange the cocktail tray, and also the coffee tray in the drawing-room. Then I bathe and change at leisure, and after that I put the hot course (or courses) in the oven, and the plates where they will get warm. If there is a hot vegetable, it is already in a colander lined with buttered paper, and I put hot water in the saucepan underneath it and leave it over very low heat indeed. I take the lettuce out of the refrigerator if there is to be a green salad, mix it carefully in a large bowl left ready in the larder with dressing ready mixed in the bottom of it, and then put the well-mixed salad into a salad dish. Finally I put coffee into the percolator, ice into a bowl, and put them on a tray with rolls or bread for the dinner-table, and butter if the first course is a cold one.

Introduction

When these things are disposed of in their appropriate places, I am at liberty to answer the telephone to the inevitable inquiries of: 'My dear, I've mislaid your letter—did you say black tie?' or 'Would it matter terribly if we're not with you until nearly eight? The children have been to a party and I haven't started to bath them yet.'

The tray which I used for the ice, percolator, etc., I leave in the dining-room for the first-course plates and dish, and take to the kitchen when I fetch the hot main course. This trayful of remains I gladly abandon on the draining-board, and after that I disregard the accumulation of plates and dishes in the dining-room. They stay there until the next morning, except for remains of food in dishes, which I collect and put away in the larder or refrigerator before I go to bed. I clear the table the next morning, and do the washing up after breakfast. Washing up is housework, and all sensible women do their housework in the morning, and never at night. I wash up the dinner-things after breakfast, which merely adds another twenty minutes or so on to the normal morning washing up. I believe that there are women who say that they simply can't go to bed while there are unwashed dishes in the sink, but this wilful assumption of the obsolete character of a brow-beaten scullery-maid I consider crazy. As for the people who dash to the sink and start splashing directly after dinner, I can only suppose that they have a dismal conviction that they will prove to be bores if they stay in the drawing-room. They are probably right.

I give this detailed description of my own arrangements for dinner-party food, because I am always deeply interested in other people's domestic arrangements, and have often modified my plans after observing someone else's short cuts to comfort and efficiency. Everyone has a method evolved to suit individual needs —trolleys for flats; special arrangements for serving-hatches and kitchen lifts; and there are even people who give their guests dinner in the kitchen. For all I know, there are people who deal with the washing up in the spirit of Pomponius Ego, who clapped the cup upon his head and threw the saucer out of window.

I have used the first person singular in describing my methods,

Introduction

in the hope of avoiding the peremptory tone used by so many writers on these matters, which can be very irritating, especially when italics are employed to enforce their views. '*Never* peel carrots, only scrape them'—that makes me smile as I hack away with a sharp knife at the leathery outsides of some very old carrots which will do perfectly well for flavouring a stew. But when I read some really ridiculous bit of didactic nonsense, such as 'White wine must *always* be served chilled', or 'It is unnecessary to make mayonnaise sauce at home, as well-known brands of it are sold everywhere', I begin to feel irritated. What quite infuriates me is the absurd use of the word 'optional', always in a highly condescending way, with a mad implication of Big Brother in the background. 'The addition of garlic is optional in a plain salad dressing.' Thank you, yes, I know that I am at liberty to put anything I choose into my salad dressing, unless I start putting hemlock into it and get involved with the coroner. This is the stage at which I feel like doing with the book what Pomponius Ego did with the saucer.

So I trust that by adhering to the first person singular I shall avoid the tiresome, authoritarian, Mother-knows-best-what-is-good-for-you tone which makes some cookery books so aggravating. When I write, 'I like spinach *en branches*, not *purée*', and 'I always make my plum puddings twelve months ahead', I do so in a spirit of conciliation, not of egoism. I have no pretentions to being an expert cook, I am merely an ardent amateur, but I consider that cooking is the one art of which it is wholly permissible to say 'I know what I like'.

Most of the hot dishes in this book are made and finished in advance, and reheated just before they are required. It is important to realize that this does not mean that they are cooked twice, and that the heat to which they are subjected must be just enough to bring them to the right temperature for serving, and never strong enough to cook the food again.

Necessary Stores

Everyone keeps a supply of essential ingredients, even in the smallest kitchenette, or else the shopping-list for a dinner would be a three-page document ending with 'two onions and a bay leaf'. I have listed the things which I try to have always available, for cooking the food described in this book. I have a store cupboard, a refrigerator, and a small larder.

In the refrigerator I keep: eggs; butter; milk; margarine; bacon (back rashers for grilling, and fat scraps which cost less than half as much); bacon-fat; dripping; hard cheese for grating; and Béchamel sauce.

In the larder there are: onions; garlic; tomatoes; carrots; turnips; lemons; parsley; celery, and pimentos, in season; and, if I can get them, fresh herbs such as chervil, chives, sage, mint, and tarragon.

In the store cupboard, on the main shelf, there are: rice; semolina; pearl barley; coarse oatmeal; plain, unbleached flour; lentils; bread-crumbs; granulated, icing, and brown sugar; spaghetti and macaroni; raisins; sultanas; mincemeat; marmalade; apricot jam; cocoa; slab chocolate; cornflour; gelatine; and olives. On the top shelf are the flavourings: dried bay leaves, sage, chervil, and mixed herbs; cloves; pepper-corns; white pepper; paprika; salt; mustard; celery salt; Marmite; powdered nutmeg; and saffron. On the bottle shelf there are: olive oil from Lucca; white wine vinegar; mushroom ketchup; red wine; white wine; port; sherry; cider; and maraschino (Drioli).

Necessary Stores

(*Notes on these items.* On a shelf by the stove I keep a pot of cooking salt and a pepper-mill filled with pepper-corns, because I use only fresh-ground black pepper when cooking, except for a few dishes which need white pepper. In the bottle shelf I keep a bottle for red wine, into which I strain what remains in the decanters, and another for white wine, but I do not put the remains of sweet white wines into this. In reserve there is dry cider as a substitute for the white, and the cheapest Algerian to supplement the red wine; and British port and British sherry, both of which are perfectly proper for cooking.)

Almost as important as the things in the larder, refrigerator and store cupboard are the contents of a drawer in the dresser. I find it well worth the trouble of assembling them from time to time. They consist of: grease-proof paper in large sheets; strong elastic bands of all sizes; little sticks sold for cocktail cherries; a ball of fine string; a paper bag full of six-inch squares of muslin and six-inch lengths of string, ready for tying up *bouquets garnis*; and one or two large squares of muslin and calico, for straining soup, etc. (If you use net or muslin curtains in your house, the best parts of worn-out ones do very well, boiled and cut up into suitable sizes. I find that it saves much time to keep a bagful of small squares of it, and short lengths of string, in readiness for the *bouquet garni* which is constantly needed.)

Batterie de Cuisine

The first cookery book I ever possessed daunted me by the assumption that I had a tool called a cutlet-bat. (It was an excellent book by the late Mrs. C. S. Peel. It was given to me by the dedicatee, and I am glad to acknowledge a debt of gratitude to both of them.) But that cutlet-bat did alarm me, by implying that an array of picturesque tools was essential for cooking even such simple things as cutlets, and I wondered if I should need a more massive bat for a fillet of beef, perhaps a mallet for the tournedos, a club for the contre-fillet, and perhaps a delicate little racquet for flattening fish. Thank goodness, I soon found that the amateur cook can use simple substitutes for most of the specialized articles demanded by the professional. A very clean milk bottle does perfectly for flattening cutlets and steak, and I use one as a rolling-pin, too, and roll the pastry on the enamelled top of my kitchen table, so that I don't need a pastry-board or pin. In fact I suspect that Victorian kitchens were as much cluttered up with unnecessary tools as are modern kitchenettes with the gadgets which salesmanship imposes on the credulous cook-hostess. Everything in this book can be cooked with the following modest list of pots and tools. (When cooking for an occasional huge party, one can borrow an extra pot and casserole for the day.)

Metal pots: a large iron pot, or other vessel with a strong base (according to the kind of stove you have); a frying-pan; an omelette pan, never used for anything else, or washed ever, but only wiped clean with paper; a double saucepan; a very large

Batterie de Cuisine

saucepan for quantities of green vegetables; one or two others of different sizes; and a fish-kettle with a strainer, but this is really not essential.

Ovenproof glass or earthenware pots: one or two large shallow dishes; one or two deep ones, with lids that fit well; a piedish or two; and six or eight small pots in which to cook an egg for each guest.

Tools: a chopping board; bowls of various sizes, one very big; a lemon squeezer; a whisk; a grater; a mincing machine; a sieve, a wire strainer, and a colander; a roasting tin and a baking tin; a draining spoon, a fish slice, and some sharp knives and some wooden spoons.

A pestle and mortar are useful, but not essential. (They can be bought cheaply in junk shops.) A weighing machine is really necessary for nervous cooks who have not learned to estimate quantities, and reassures them. A pressure-cooker is very convenient, but one can get on very well without one. No doubt electric mixers and mincers are invaluable, but as to that I can't say.

The storage of supplies in the kitchen cupboard can be organized very simply by using glass jars. I once read an article by a woman journalist who complained that if the groceries she bought were not in cellophane bags she was apt to mistake their contents, and to confuse the ground ginger with curry powder and to put icing sugar into the sauce when she wanted cornflour; and she added that she was for ever upsetting packets of cereals and other things because they were so easily upset by a hand thrust hastily into the cupboard where they stood. This grumble left me with a nightmare vision of a shelf full of overturned packets and paper bags spilling their contents on to an existing layer of musty, mouldy oatmeal and currants and cornflour and prunes. For the first time, I felt that there was something to be said for wasting money on rows of expensive kitchen jars prettily stamped with the names of their contents, although I had always thought that fad of the fussy cook-hostess made her kitchen resemble an old-fashioned chemist's shop, which is the last idea that a kitchen should suggest.

Batterie de Cuisine

Very clean glass jars are the perfect answer to the two extreme absurdities of shiftless muddle or the prim provision of an apothecary's pots. One-pound jam jars hold everything bought in small quantities, such as cloves and herbs and ground ginger. Two-pound jars hold comfortably a pound of dry cereals or fruit. Large storage jars are needed for things used in greater quantities, such as sugar and rice. They can be covered with the metal tops once-used for fruit bottling and then washed—they clip on fairly tightly and keep out the dust which gets into the kitchen cupboard with the best-fitting door. It is important to give each jar its appointed place and to keep it there, so that habit combines with the senses to make it impossible to confuse like-looking substances with each other.

In the refrigerator, it is essential to keep things covered, especially all liquids. The evaporation from uncovered liquids makes the whole thing into that tiresome blizzard which obliges one to defrost it. Dressed salad soon becomes uneatable if put into the refrigerator. Fresh lettuce or other salad material, on the contrary, stays crisp for days if washed, put into a polythene bag, and kept in the refrigerator. Roast meat loses all flavour, but stews in a covered casserole do not suffer, and should be kept there in hot weather. I keep the wrapping-papers of butter and margarine in the refrigerator, in a paper bag. Remains of soup are kept there, in a covered jam jar.

Soup with a vegetable content, not kept in the refrigerator, must be brought to the boil once in every twenty-four hours if it is not used, or it will go bad. Cooked potatoes go bad very soon, but will keep for several days, covered, in the refrigerator. If you put a cut melon into the refrigerator, cover it with two polythene bags.

Certain simple, essential preparations are referred to so often in the recipes in this book that it seems more sensible to give an account of them here than to scatter them about in the index, as it would be absurd to repeat the easy formulae each time they are mentioned. There are five of them.

BOUQUET GARNI. Mine consists of a clove of garlic crushed firmly with the blade of a knife, two cloves, six peppercorns, a bay

Batterie de Cuisine

leaf, a sprig of parsley, and one of thyme, tied up with string in a bit of muslin. The thyme is not essential, although an improvement.

MARINADE. Oil, white wine vinegar, or lemon juice, chopped onion and garlic, and a pinch of chopped herbs, stirred together and used for steeping meat or fish to give it flavour.

COURT BOUILLON. A chopped onion and carrot and stick of celery and perhaps mushroom stalks are cooked in white wine and water with salt and pepper and a piece of lemon peel and a *bouquet garni* for half an hour, to make a *cuisson* in which to poach fish. Red wine must be used if the fish is to be cooked *au bleu*.

FUMET. The Court Bouillon, after the fish has been removed, boiled up again with the bones and trimmings and much reduced. It should be strained through a cloth, and will jellify.

ROUX. A white roux is made by putting a spoonful of butter into a saucepan and stirring a spoonful of flour into it until it spreads and bubbles over gentle heat. A brown roux is made by letting this mixture cook longer, stirring all the time to ensure that it does not stick to the pan and burn, until it is decidedly brown.

ASPIC. Powdered gelatine is sold in packets which contain enough to set a pint of liquid. I make aspic with three-quarters of a pint of vegetable *consommé* (see p. 31) and make up the rest of the pint with sherry.

POINTS TO REMEMBER

To peel tomatoes (you almost always have to), put them into boiling water for a minute, and then the skin will come off very easily.

To clarify fat, put hot fat into a bowl and pour cold water on it, and stir. Put cold fat, soup skimmings, etc., into a bowl and pour boiling water on it and stir. In both cases the fat will form a cake on the surface when cold, and can be removed, chilled, and scraped free of the deposit on its under side. The smaller the bowl, the thicker and more manageable the cake of fat. I use it as dripping.

Batterie de Cuisine

Throughout this book, when I say 'a spoonful', I mean a tablespoonful of liquid, and a heaped-up tablespoonful of solids.

Butter is better than the best margarine for cooking, but margarine can be substituted for most uses, if it must be, except for puff pastry and sauces.

Oven heat. The figures given for oven heat—in degrees Fahrenheit, and Gas Regulo numbers—apply to the part of the oven in which this heat obtains. Some ovens, such as gas ones, are hottest at the top, and it is no good putting the dish to be cooked at the bottom of the oven and expecting it to cook or heat up in the time given for the maximum use of the heat recommended.

I always put a large shallow dish or plate full of water in the bottom of the oven when reheating food. The steam which it produces makes the heat moist and the food is less likely to lose any of its moisture while it is being reheated.

Dishes of cooked rice or barley sometimes form a brown crust on the surface if reheated a little too long in the oven. This crust is delicious, and I stir it into the dish with a fork before it comes to the table.

Flower-pots make useful substitutes for a refrigerator, for chilling things in small containers, and for keeping them cool. The well-scrubbed flower-pot is submerged in cold water for five minutes, then used to cover a sauce or pudding in a bowl. The pot will evaporate for about twelve hours, and the air inside it will stay cold for that time. Then, if necessary, it must be soaked in cold water again.

Sauces

BÉCHAMEL SAUCE

Béchamel is the basic sauce, the simplest expression of the French genius for making raw material into something delicious. It was not until I had learned to make it properly, quickly, and without anxiety that I felt that I had begun to cook.

I always make it in a double saucepan, with water simmering in the bottom one. It takes rather less time to make it in a small single pan, but then it must be stirred all the time, whereas in the double pan it thickens with an occasional stir, while I do something else.

The materials for all thick sauces are: one ounce of flour, one ounce of butter, and half a pint of liquid. There is no permissible variation of this formula, although the flour may be plain flour, cornflour, or rice flour, the butter may, at a pinch, be margarine, and the liquid milk, or any form of stock or vegetable *cuisson*.

When I make Béchamel sauce, I put into my double saucepan as much butter as I can scoop up with a tablespoon. (This is as near an ounce as makes no difference.) When the butter is melting, I put into it a heaped-up tablespoonful of plain white flour, and stir the butter and flour together with a wooden spoon until they combine and begin to spread on the bottom of the pan. Then I leave this mixture to bubble very gently for three minutes, while half a pint of milk is warming in another pan. When the butter and flour have consolidated into a *roux*, I remove the top pot to the table and pour into it a little of the warm milk, stir this in until it

Sauces

is smoothly absorbed, and add the rest of the milk by degrees and make sure as I stir it in that there are no lumps. (The lump on the back of the spoon has to be scraped off against the side of the pan, and carefully stirred into the sauce.) Then the top pot is put back on the lower one, and the sauce is seasoned with salt, pepper, and a squeeze of lemon juice. It is then left to cook with an occasional stir until it is thick enough.

This essential sauce may be seasoned with all sorts of other things, such as crushed garlic, onion juice, nutmeg, crushed herbs, tomato *purée*, grated cheese, or pounded anchovy. When I make a Béchamel I often make twice as much as I need, and put the surplus half in the refrigerator, in a covered bowl. It can be reheated in the bowl over hot water in a saucepan, and seasoning added to it as it heats.

I read lately, in a very popular English women's periodical, the following instructions for making a sauce. 'Take three-quarters of a pint of milk, use two tablespoonfuls to mix with a tablespoonful of cornflour to a smooth paste. Bring the rest of the milk to the boil and pour it on to the paste, stirring well. Return to the saucepan, bring to the boil, season, add two ounces of margarine, stir until well blended, simmer for three minutes.'

I did this. I had always wanted to know just how the nasty English White Sauce was made, and now I do know. The result was just what I had expected it to be. It contrived to be both pasty and greasy in an overall consistency of slime, and it took exactly four minutes less time to make than it takes to make a Béchamel in the orthodox way. The proportions are strangely and perversely different from the correct proportions—the comparison is interesting.

English White Sauce	*Béchamel Sauce*
1 oz. of flour	1 oz. of flour
2 oz. of margarine	1 oz. of butter
¾ pint of milk	½ pint of milk

I cannot guess how these odd proportions were arrived at, or why it was thought advisable to put the butter (or margarine) in last. It seems to me to be a deliberate departure from a simple method

Sauces

of cooking a simple thing, resulting in something so nasty that it can scarcely be compared with the original. I suspect that in the majority of English kitchens it is known as 'the easy way' to make a sauce. Now that I have done it myself I am prepared to assert that it isn't easy, and that it isn't a sauce.

POULETTE SAUCE

I make this sauce in the same way that I make a Béchamel, except that I use veal broth, or chicken broth instead of milk for some dishes. While it is thickening in the double saucepan, I stir up the yolk of one egg with the juice of half a lemon (for half a pint of sauce). When the sauce is cooked, I take it off the fire and stir the egg into it, and also about two spoonfuls of cream. The pan is then returned to the gentle heat of just simmering water in the bottom pot, and the sauce is whisked with a wire whisk for a few minutes. This splendid sauce is especially good with mussels.

VELOUTÉ SAUCE

I use for this, half a pint of Béchamel sauce, and half a pint of veal broth (see p. 36) which has been carefully made, highly seasoned, and skimmed of its fat when cold. The Béchamel and the broth are stirred together in a double saucepan until they are thoroughly blended. This sauce coagulates well when cold, and is useful for masking things which are to be served cold.

WHITE SAUCE FOR CHICKEN OR VEAL

This sauce is made in the same way as a Béchamel, except that chicken broth (see p. 37) or veal broth (see p. 36) is used instead of milk, and a spoonful or two of cream is added when it is cooked.

WHITE SAUCE FOR FISH

This sauce is made in the same way as a Béchamel, except that the liquid is the *court bouillon* in which the fish has been cooked.

Sauces

It is finished with half a spoonful of butter which is stirred into it off the fire, and the sauce is not heated again after this addition.

SOUBISE SAUCE

Half a pint of Béchamel sauce is required for this, and it is made (or warmed) while the onions are cooking. I chop very small half a pound of onions and cook them very gently in about two spoonfuls of water, shaking the covered pan frequently, until they are pulp, and have absorbed the water, and then I add a spoonful of butter, and salt and pepper, and stir them until they have absorbed all the butter. After that they are pressed through a wire sieve into the pan containing the warmed Béchamel, and the resulting *purée* is stirred together.

TOMATO SAUCE

I cut up a pound of ripe tomatoes (skinned), with a chopped onion and clove of garlic, add a bay leaf, and stir them in a saucepan over the lowest possible heat, without any additional liquid, until they are all squashy and cooking very gently in their own juice. I then put in salt and pepper, and leave them to simmer, giving an occasional stir, while I make a brown *roux* in a double saucepan. This entails cooking a spoonful of butter and one of flour, stirring all the time, until the *roux* is decidedly brown. When it is dark enough, and the tomatoes are reduced to a thick pulp (without having ever been allowed to stick to the bottom of their pan), the tomato pulp, minus the bay leaf, is pressed through a wire strainer into the *roux*, and returned to the heat of the bottom saucepan and stirred until it is thick. There is all the difference in the world between this tomato sauce and the stuff bought in bottles.

MADEIRA SAUCE

I make this with a brown *roux*, and stir into it half a pint of strong meat stock, or vegetable *consommé* (see p. 31). When it

Sauces

is perfectly smooth, I put the top pot back on the simmering water in the bottom pot, and add to the sauce a spoonful of tomato *purée* and three spoonfuls of Madeira, with salt and pepper and a *bouquet garni*. Well stirred, the sauce is then left to cook, with an occasional stir, until it is really thick. Then the bouquet is taken out.

MAYONNAISE SAUCE

I put the yolks of two eggs and a teaspoonful of lemon juice into a bowl with a pinch of salt and four grinds of pepper and stir them with a fork until they are mixed. Then I drop olive oil into the bowl a few drops at a time, and go on stirring and dropping until the sauce is thick enough. It is kept in the refrigerator until it is wanted.

SAUCE VERTE

I make a mayonnaise sauce, and add to it a small handful of spinach or watercress which, with a little parsley, has been chopped, pounded, and pressed through a wire sieve. The raw greenstuff is carefully stirred into the mayonnaise, and makes a most excellent sauce.

CUMBERLAND SAUCE

I detest this sauce, and so I make it rapidly and recklessly with the ingredients used in quite random proportions. They are port, red-currant jelly, and thick made-mustard, and I stir them all together with energetic disgust, and the result is always a success with cold pork, ham, or goose.

PARSNIP SAUCE

I peel and cut up a large parsnip, and simmer it in half a pint of salted water until it is soft. It is then pressed through a wire sieve until it is a watery *purée* with its liquid, which must be made

Sauces

up to half a pint, if necessary, with the addition of milk. This is then stirred into a white *roux* until it is perfectly smooth, and returned to the heat of the under-saucepan, and has the juice of half a lemon added to it, and six grinds of the pepper-mill. It is cooked until it is decidedly thick.

This is an interesting sauce, the lemon juice combining with the sweetish flavour of the parsnip to produce a sweet-sour taste, and it makes a good dressing for vegetables or chicken, and for the stuffing of cold vegetable dishes such as peppers. If it is to be served hot, the addition of a little cream is an improvement.

TARTARE SAUCE

If I can get fresh herbs for this sauce, I chop very small a bunch of parsley, some sprigs of tarragon and lemon balm and chervil, and then pound them with a gherkin and two boned anchovies and a teaspoonful of mustard and a good pinch of salt and four grinds of the pepper-mill. If I can't get fresh herbs, I use dried ones, and soak them for an hour in very little lemon juice. When all is well pounded, I stir four spoonfuls of olive oil into the mixture. Then I beat up two egg yolks with a spoonful of wine vinegar, and whisk this mixture into the other one, and whisk briskly with a wire whisk until it is all frothy. Then I chill it in the refrigerator until I need it.

HOLLANDAISE SAUCE

For this most useful sauce I beat up four ounces of butter until it is soft and creamy, and then I add the yolks of four eggs and beat until they are mixed thoroughly with the butter, then the juice of half a lemon and a pinch of paprika, and, lastly, a cupful of hot water stirred in gradually. When all is well stirred, I put it over low heat in a double saucepan and go on stirring until it is as thick as thick cream. It is as good cold as it is hot.

Soup

Soup in England is supposed to be either thick or clear. (Although there is the third kind, which is neither, and which is called Gravy Soup.) The thick kind is liable to be simply gruel; and the thin variety usually consists of some warm water flavoured with dissolved meat-cube. It may, however, be diversified by the addition of some tapioca (so suggestive of frogs' spawn) or of some strands of the pasta aptly named vermicelli. Shrinking from the prospect of pond-life or sick-room 'slops', the housewife tends to open tins instead, and this seems a pity, because it is very easy to make soup which is more interesting, more nourishing, and much cheaper than anything out of a tin.

VEGETABLE CONSOMMÉ

An iron pot or other thick saucepan should be used for this, and two spoonfuls of bacon fat or dripping made hot in it. Then half a pound of onions, half a pound of carrots, one turnip, half a parsnip and a stick of celery, all chopped, are melted in the fat and cooked until they are fairly coloured but not browned. Then a quart of hot water is added, with salt, pepper, and a *bouquet garni*. The soup is skimmed when it boils, and then allowed to simmer for two hours very gently. It is then strained into a bowl, the fat removed from the surface when it is cold, and the soup heated again and strained through a cloth to make it really clear. It is improved by the addition of sherry when reheating.

Soup

TOMATO SOUP

I make this with the tomatoes which are very cheap because they are too squashy, or too small, for salad purposes. It is a useful ingredient for various dishes as well as being a good soup.

Having boiled a chopped onion and clove of garlic rapidly in a cupful of water for a few minutes, I put in a pound of tomatoes cut up, another cupful of water, and salt and pepper. The saucepan lid should be a good fit, and the soup should simmer for an hour. It is then pressed through a wire sieve, all but the tomato skins. This makes enough for four people, and it is an improvement to put a spoonful of cream on the top of each helping.

LETTUCE AND POTATO SOUP

I make this with the coarse outside leaves of a large lettuce, either a cos or a round one. They are cooked with one big cut-up potato in a pint of water with salt, pepper and a *bouquet garni*, very gently for an hour in a saucepan with a tight-fitting lid. The *bouquet* is then removed, the soup pressed through a wire sieve, and finished with a little cream stirred into it when it is reheated.

WHITE ONION SOUP I

Two large Spanish onions, chopped small, are melted in an iron pot or other thick saucepan in two ounces of butter, and stirred until they are golden but not brown. Then a quart of veal stock is added, with salt, pepper and a bay leaf, and the soup is simmered for half an hour, and then pressed through a wire sieve (after the bay leaf has been removed). Little *croûtons* of fried bread are the orthodox accompaniment.

WHITE ONION SOUP II

This is a very thick soup. Six small white onions are minced and then cooked very gently for an hour in a cupful of milk and

Soup

a cupful of water, with salt, pepper, two cloves and a piece of lemon peel. The saucepan-lid must fit tightly. The cloves and lemon peel are removed, and a little cream stirred into the soup when reheating it.

OFF-WHITE ONION SOUP

Two large Spanish onions, chopped small, are cooked in hot oil until they are pale brown, being stirred all the time to prevent them burning. A quart of vegetable stock is then added, with salt, pepper, and a small handful of chopped parsley. When it boils, two spoonfuls of semolina are sprinkled into it gradually while it is stirred to prevent the semolina forming any lumps. The whole thing is then turned into a double saucepan and simmered for an hour, after which it is pressed through a wire sieve. A spoonful of tomato *purée* is added and stirred thoroughly into the soup when it is reheated.

BROSE

This is the stuff that makes the Scots so strong. I make it with the *cuisson* of any green vegetables, or of any roots except potatoes. (I use the word *cuisson* because cabbage-water sounds revolting, although, in fact, I consider it delicious.)

Having measured the *cuisson*, I put it into a double saucepan with pepper, a bay leaf, and as much more salt as it seems to need. When it bubbles, I sprinkle into it a spoonful of coarse oatmeal for each half-pint, stir it well for a few minutes, and let it simmer, closely covered, for two hours. It is then pressed through a wire sieve until nothing remains in the sieve but the bay leaf, care having been taken to get all the oatmeal through. It is finished with a little cream when being reheated. This is an excellent smooth soup, especially good when made with the *cuisson* of leeks or brussels sprouts.

MUSHROOM SOUP

I use a quarter of a pound of mushrooms for this, stalks and

Soup

all. The mushrooms are broken up small, and the stalks chopped finely, and all are cooked in a spoonful of bacon fat and two spoonfuls of water, in a small pan which is shaken frequently for twenty minutes. Salt, pepper, and a spoonful of chopped parsley are added half-way through the cooking. Meanwhile, I make a brown *roux* with a spoonful of butter and one of flour, and stir into it a pint of hot veal stock, with salt, pepper, and a squeeze of lemon juice. When it is cooked, I put the mushrooms and their fatty *cuisson* into this, and stir it until it thickens to the right consistency.

LENTIL SOUP

I make this when I have a lot of bacon rinds. First they are put in the bottom of the oven in a dish and left to melt while something else is cooking, with the result that they are partly frizzled and there is some bacon fat to add to the pot in the refrigerator. Then they are tied together with string in a bundle.

I soak four ounces of lentils in cold water overnight, and drain them. A chopped onion and clove of garlic are melted in hot bacon fat, and the drained lentils are then stirred into it and cooked for a minute or two. A pint of hot potato *cuisson* is then added, with salt (as required) and pepper and a good pinch of dried sage. The bundle of frizzled bacon rinds is put in when all is well mixed together, the lid put tightly on the pot, and the soup simmered for an hour. The bundle is removed before the soup is pressed through a wire sieve.

POTATO SOUP

A pound of peeled, cut-up potatoes, a finely chopped onion and clove of garlic, a sprig of fresh mint, two cloves and a piece of lemon peel are cooked gently in a pint of water, with salt and pepper, for half an hour. Then the cloves and lemon peel are removed, the soup pressed through a wire sieve, and when it is reheated a little cream and several small bits of butter are stirred into it.

Soup

SALAD SOUP

When I have to make a big dish of salad of a comprehensive kind, I keep for soup everything that will not quite do for the salad—the outside leaves of lettuce, odd bits of watercress and tomato and celery and carrot and radish, parsley stalks, the tops of chives and spring onions, the tender pods of very young peas and broad beans. I break up the lettuce, chop everything else small, skin the tomatoes, and add a chopped clove of garlic or two, and a chopped onion if there is not much tops of chives or spring onions. Two handfuls of this mixed vegetable stuff are cooked in a quart of cold water with salt and pepper and a handful of rice which has been washed and drained. It is done when the carrot and celery are soft.

LATVIAN SOUP

I use a big saucepan for this, and put into it a handful of fat-bacon scraps, cut up, and let them colour over gentle heat until plenty of the fat has come out. Then two onions, chopped very small, and two finely minced cloves of garlic are stirred with the bacon until they are melted and just beginning to colour. Then three skinned chopped tomatoes are added, and left to cook for a few minutes with an occasional stir while I chop very small three sticks of celery, one peeled cooking apple, and half a small cabbage. These are added to the well-stirred contents of the pan, and hot water is poured in—enough to come three parts of the way up it. Four ounces of washed rice is then added, a handful of washed sultanas, and plenty of salt, pepper, and grated nutmeg. When it has come to the boil, it is allowed to simmer gently until everything is cooked. It has to be stirred from time to time, so that the apple, which soon dissolves into a *purée*, mixes well with the rice and they both absorb the fat while cooking. If, when the soup is finished, it seems too sour, this can be corrected by putting in a little brown sugar and cooking for a few moments longer.

Soup

VEAL BROTH

This broth, which is rather dull on its own, is the strong and nourishing basis of many of the white soups that require a meat stock, and is also the basis of excellent sauces. It is made with veal bones—either the knuckle bone from which the meat has been cut for a dish, or with the veal bones sold by the butcher for soup. In either case the butcher ought to chop them into manageable-sized pieces.

An iron pot or other strong saucepan is needed. Two spoonfuls of oil or dripping should be made hot in it, and a sliced onion browned in that, before the veal bones go in. They have to be cooked until they are slightly coloured, being moved about so that they are evenly done. Then enough hot water is poured in to cover them, a few slices of carrot, turnip and parsnip, some bits of parsley, a slice of lemon peel, a *bouquet garni*, and plenty of salt and pepper, and the water is brought gently to the boil. The broth is then skimmed and simmered for two hours. It is strained, and the bones are saved for making another stock in the same way. Both first and second veal stocks should jellify. The first stock is the one with which to make veal soup, as it has more flavour of the meat than the second stock, which is useful for sauces. The fat must of course be removed from the surface when the strained stock is cold.

CREAMED VEAL SOUP

I chop small a clove of garlic, a bit of celery root, and a small shallot, and pound them with a lot of parsley stalks, the juice of half a lemon, and a pinch of nutmeg. When all is well pounded, I put the stuff into a pint of hot veal stock, and let it simmer for a few minutes. Meanwhile a white *roux* is prepared with a spoonful of butter and one of flour. When the *roux* is cooked, the veal stock is strained into it carefully by degrees, and the soup is simmered until it is cooked and thick enough. (If this soup is made in advance, and allowed to cool before it is reheated, it

Soup

should be left in its saucepan and the top of the pan covered tightly with wet greaseproof paper while it is hot. This will prevent a skin forming on it.) When reheating, two spoonfuls of cream are stirred into it.

BROWN VEAL SOUP

A brown veal broth is necessary for this soup. To produce this, I use rather more fat when making the broth, and let the onion get brown without burning, and then brown a tomato and the slices of roots in the fat at the same time as the bones, which are kept moving in the sizzling vegetables until they are decidedly brown before the water is added.

The soup is made in the same way as the Creamed Veal Soup, except that a brown *roux* is made, instead of a white one, and a spoonful of Madeira is used instead of lemon juice.

CHICKEN BROTH

I make this with the carcass of a cooked chicken, broken up and browned in a large strong saucepan with an onion in two spoonfuls of hot dripping or bacon fat. Then I put in a quart of hot water and a *bouquet garni* and plenty of salt and pepper and simmer it for three hours very gently indeed. It is then strained, the fat removed from the top when it is cold, and it is heated again and then strained through a cloth.

This is plain chicken broth—too plain, without additions. It is, however, delicious if, when reheated, a spoonful each of raw grated (or minced) onion, carrot, and celery are stirred into it.

COLD CHICKEN SOUP

If the chicken broth made according to the foregoing recipe is strong enough to jellify, it will do very well for a cold soup. I stir the raw grated vegetables into it while it is hot, and stir again when it is nearly cold in order to distribute them thoroughly, and then turn the soup into soup-cups to set.

Soup

CREAMED CHICKEN SOUP

If I have no chicken broth, I use the *cuisson* from a boiled chicken for this soup. I flavour it with a sprig of fresh chervil pounded with a clove of garlic and the juice of half a lemon. This is strained into a pint of the broth and simmered for a few minutes while a white *roux* is made with a spoonful of butter and one of flour. When the *roux* is cooked, the broth is stirred into it gradually, and simmered in the double saucepan until it is thick. If prepared in advance, it is covered well with wet greaseproof paper to prevent a skin forming. Two spoonfuls of cream are stirred into it when reheating.

GAME SOUP

The carcasses of goose, duck, or pigeon do as well for this soup as those of game birds. I break up the carcass and brown the pieces in hot dripping or bacon fat with a chopped onion until it is all well coloured. Then I put in enough hot water to cover it completely, and salt and pepper and a *bouquet garni*, and a teaspoonful of grated root ginger, and a glass of port. When it has come to the boil, it is skimmed, and then simmered gently for two hours, after which it is strained into a bowl, and the top fat removed when it is cold. This stock is measured, and a brown *roux* made with a spoonful of butter and one of flour for a pint of stock, or a bigger *roux* in proportion to the amount of liquid. The stock is heated, and added gradually to the *roux* when that is ready. It should need no further flavouring. Like all thick soups, it should be covered when hot with wet greaseproof paper to prevent a skin forming on it.

HARE SOUP

I make this soup when I have cooked a hare and then cut off the meat for some made-dish, so that the bones remain. Several large pieces of fat bacon are put into a strong pan, and when they

Soup

have coloured and the fat has come out, the bones and carcass of the hare (broken up) are browned in the fat with a chopped onion, carrot, and turnip. The liver is chopped, and added, and a glass of red wine is poured in, and then the heat is reduced while the cooking continues for another five minutes. Then hot water is added—enough to cover it all completely, and salt, pepper, a *bouquet garni*, and a pinch of mixed spice. When it boils it is skimmed, and then it simmers for three hours, after which it is strained into a bowl, and the fat removed when it is cold. For a pint of the stock, a brown *roux* is made with a spoonful of butter and one of flour, and the heated stock stirred into the *roux* when it is ready. It is finished with a spoonful of cream and one of chopped parsley, well stirred in.

OXTAIL SOUP

I make this with the remains of a dish of braised oxtail (see p. 93). There are usually a few of the little bones left, and I cut the meat off these, and scrape the remains of sauce and vegetables from the dish into a saucepan with the bits of meat, and blend it all with a pint of hot vegetable *cuisson*. It is all stirred and heated until it is perfectly smooth, a spoonful of port is added, and a little more salt and pepper if that seems necessary.

FISH SOUP

Fish soup, once a common English dish, is now considered odd and foreign. It is surely time that we took to it again, for fish, with its bones full of glue and its flesh full of flavour, is an excellent material for soup.

I make this soup when I have a *court bouillon* left after poaching fish, and don't want to make a *fumet*. I put the bones and trimmings of the fish into the *court bouillon* with a skinned, chopped tomato, a small spoonful of oil, and a pinch of saffron, and simmer it for half an hour in a covered pan. For each pint of this liquid, I mix in a cup a teaspoonful of cornflour with enough cold milk to make a smooth cream. This is stirred into the warm soup,

Soup

which is then cooked for a few minutes until the cornflour is thoroughly blended with it, then strained into another pan and simmered until it is of a proper thickness. Finally, chopped parsley is added.

HERRING SOUP

Two herrings, cleaned and scaled but not boned, are chopped up roughly and cooked in a spoonful of oil with a chopped onion and clove of garlic over brisk heat for a few minutes and stirred and mashed all the time. Then a peeled, cut-up tomato is put in and stirred for another minute or two, and salt and pepper are sprinkled over it all. Then a spoonful of flour is stirred in until the oily juice is absorbed. A pint of hot potato *cuisson* is poured over the mixture and stirred until it boils, the lid is put on and it is left to simmer for three-quarters of an hour. The soup is then put through a hair sieve (a wire one allows the small bones to get through) and finished with chopped parsley and a little cream.

FINNAN HADDOCK SOUP

A strange and delicious soup can be made with the bones and trimmings of a dried haddock that has been cooked for breakfast, if the fish is filleted after cooking so that the bones are available for the soup. Put them with the trimmings (the head, tail, fins, etc.) into a saucepan with the *cuisson* from the cooking, and make it up with water to a pint. I add a slice of onion, a piece of lemon peel, a *bouquet garni*, pepper and a little salt, and simmer it for an hour in a tightly covered pan. It is then strained.

PANADA

Four slices of fresh white bread, a chopped onion and clove of garlic, a spoonful of grated cheese and a pinch of saffron are simmered in a pint of milk and water for half an hour, with celery-salt and pepper. The soup is then pressed through a wire sieve, and served with little sprigs of fresh watercress. It has a peculiar texture which some people loathe.

Soup

BROWN MUTTON BROTH

For this I use the bones and bits of fat which I have trimmed off breast or neck of mutton or lamb. I put them with a large chopped onion and clove of garlic in a pan over brisk heat, and move it all about so that the fat melts and the onion gets browned and the bones begin to sizzle. Then I put in enough hot water to cover them, with salt and pepper and a bay leaf and a pinch of dried sage, and a small handful of pearl barley. (This is for about a pint of water. I use more barley if there are a lot of bones, and more liquid to cover them.) It is brought slowly to the boil, skimmed, and simmered for an hour and a half. Then I strain it into a bowl, remove from the strainer all the bits of meat and bones and the *bouquet*, and put the barley back into the soup. When it is cold, the barley will have sunk, and the fat can be removed from the surface. When reheating this soup, I put into it bits of any cooked vegetables that I may have, such as carrots, peas, beans, and bits of boiled potato. If by any chance I have over-browned the bones and that has given the broth a slightly bitter taste, I correct that by putting in a skinned, chopped tomato and a spoonful of brown sugar and cooking it for a few minutes more.

SOUP MADE WITH REMAINS

The things that remain in the corners of dishes—spoonfuls of stew, risotto, pasta, gnocchi, vegetables, sauce—can be made into good soup with any vegetable *cuisson*, or second stock from the bones of meat or fowls. Stir whatever remains you have, very gently, into a pint of stock until it simmers and thickens, with more salt and pepper if necessary. If it is not thick enough, put in a teaspoonful of cornflour mixed to a cream with milk, and cook a little longer. Flavour, if it seems dull, with lemon juice, or nutmeg, or tomato *purée*.

Eggs

It seems to be a current fashion to regard eggs as suitable for a first course at luncheon, but not at dinner. This seems to me great nonsense. Until quite lately it was an English habit to serve hard-boiled eggs, stuffed, as a savoury course at dinner, and personally I would very much rather begin my dinner with a hot, soft egg, deliciously cooked, than end it with a cold, slippery hard one tasting disagreeably of anchovy paste. It may be said that one is overdoing the proteins by having eggs before meat, but after all a dinner-party is a small feast, not a balanced meal for undergrown orphans. I trust that I shall never entertain a calorie-counter unawares.

In the summer, cold soft eggs in aspic or a suitable sauce make an excellent and convenient first course, I find. Much as I like omelettes I never have them at parties because of the practical difficulties of making them at the right moment. I think it is important to buy only the best eggs. Small eggs upset the proportions of a recipe, and look miserly when cooked—and cheap eggs are either small, or stale, or even both.

OEUFS MOLLETS. Most of the eggs in the following recipes are the soft-boiled eggs which are called *œufs mollets*. They are boiled for exactly six minutes, and then shelled with great care, because the whites are hard and the yolks soft inside. They must be shelled at once, or the heat of the shell will go on cooking them. When shelled, they can be kept for some time in a dish of hot water

Eggs

(about as hot as a baby's bath-water) well covered in a warm place. I find it advisable to take eggs out of the refrigerator an hour or two before boiling them, because the shell of an icy egg often cracks when put into boiling water.

COLD EGGS IN A PURÉE OF CARROT TOPS

For this dish I use the tops of young carrots, delicious greenstuff which is usually thrown away. (They must be really young carrots, because the tops of old ones taste bitter.) I wash two handfuls of the tops, remove the stalks, and cook them in a pint of water with a handful of coarse oatmeal, a chopped onion, salt and pepper and a spoonful of tomato *purée*. When it is cooked, this mixture is pressed through a wire sieve, and used, when cold, as a sauce for *œufs mollets*, which are put in separate small dishes and covered with the sauce. A small blob of whipped cream very slightly flavoured with lemon juice and onion juice is put on top of each one.

EGGS AND HAM IN ASPIC

I put a small slice of ham into each separate dish—lean ham, preferably rather overcooked, so that it is dry and crumbly—and put an *œuf mollet* on each slice. Aspic (see p. 23) is poured over them when it is pretty cool, and when it has set, the surface is decorated with a sprinkling of chopped gherkins.

COLD EGGS IN FISH ASPIC

I make this when I have a *court bouillon* and the bones and trimmings of the fish that was cooked in it. It is reduced to a *fumet*, strained carefully through a cloth to make it very clear, and when cold it ought to set. If it doesn't, it has to be heated again with enough gelatine to set it. The jelly is put into the refrigerator to get firm, and then chopped small. Cold *œufs mollets* are arranged on a dish surrounded with little cubes of cucumber —plenty of them—and the chopped aspic is spread over it all, and the dish kept in the refrigerator until it is wanted.

Eggs

COLD EGGS IN GREEN MAYONNAISE

Oeufs mollets are put into separate dishes and covered with plenty of *sauce verte* (see p. 29) and decorated with sprigs of watercress.

HOT BAKED EGGS AND BACON

A shallow ovenproof dish is buttered, and then a spoonful of cream is poured into it, and the dish tilted about until the cream has coated the bottom. Fresh eggs are then broken into the dish, with care to ensure that they stay as separate as possible. Chopped peeled tomatoes, and chives or shallots chopped very small, are put between the eggs, and the surface is salted and peppered. Then, for each egg, a rasher of bacon is cut into one-inch squares and these are spread over everything, very gently in order not to break the eggs. Cream is then poured over the dish—two spoonfuls for each egg—and plenty of chopped parsley sprinkled over it. It is baked in a medium oven (350 deg., Gas, No. 4) for twenty minutes. This dish can be prepared an hour before dinner and left ready to put into the oven twenty minutes before it is wanted. Chopped mushrooms and softish cheese (fresh Cheddar or Cheshire) can be substituted for the tomatoes and chives, to make a slightly different but equally good course.

It is a wonderful breakfast dish, but of course chives, shallots and cheese must be kept out of it, since the Island Race cannot stomach these flavours before the sun is over the yard-arm. (This is an odd fad for people whose forebears breakfasted on chops and ale, and I must say I think it is rather ridiculous. Give me a bit of garlicky foreign sausage at any hour of the day, rather than the dreary modern British banger that tastes of nothing much except pork fat and stale bread.)

COLD BAKED EGGS

Baked eggs which are to be eaten hot can be done with milk,

Eggs

but when they are to be served cold, cream has to be used, or they will be watery.

For six eggs, I seed and cut up into fairly small pieces, two pimentos, and melt them in a spoonful of oil over low heat for a few minutes until they are soft, moving them about so that they do not stick. They are then removed with a draining-spoon, and a quarter of a pound of mushrooms, broken up, is cooked in the same oil very gently until they are getting soft. All these pieces are then cooled on a sieve to ensure that they are well drained. Six small ovenproof dishes are buttered, and a teaspoonful of cream is put into each one, and the dish turned until the cream coats it. A fresh egg is broken into each dish, salted and peppered, and then the pieces of pimento and mushroom are slipped in all round the sides, with care to avoid breaking the yolks of the eggs. A spoonful of cream is then put into each dish, and they are baked in a medium oven (340 deg., Gas, No. 4) for twenty minutes. They are served cold, decorated with little pieces of raw pimento kept back for this purpose. (Fresh pimentos, red, yellow or green, are used for this dish, as the tinned ones are too wet.)

BAKED SPANISH OMELETTE

I find this a convenient dish to cook for supper after the theatre, because most of the preparations can be made beforehand. In the morning I chop up small, some carrots, turnip, celery, onion, pimento, garlic and potato, and cook them gently in oil in a big pan until they are soft. The potatoes are put in last because they are cooked the soonest. Salt and pepper are added during the cooking, and the vegetables are stirred very often to prevent them sticking. They are drained well on a sieve, and a few cooked peas are added, either fresh ones or small tinned ones. Well mixed together, all the vegetables are turned into an ample shallow ovenproof dish which has been well buttered, so that they cover the bottom to the depth of about an inch. Two or three raw peeled tomatoes are cut in pieces and added. This dish is left on the kitchen table, with eggs, butter, and a bowl containing chopped parsley and cold water. For each person, two eggs are provided,

Eggs

and rather more than half a spoonful of water is measured into the bowl. Salt, the pepper-mill, and the egg-whisk are left ready.

As soon as I return from the theatre, I put the oven on at a strong heat, and put the dish into it on the upper shelf. Then I break the eggs into the bowl containing the water and the chopped parsley, add salt and pepper, whisk them a little, and then put in, while whisking, quite a lot of butter in little bits—at least a good spoonful for four eggs. When they are well beaten, I take the dish out of the oven and pour the eggs over the vegetables, lower the oven heat to 350 deg. (Gas, No. 4) and put the dish back. It is left there for exactly twenty minutes to cook, which affords a convenient opportunity for me to have a drink with my guests.

I use other vegetables in their season for this omelette, such as broad beans, French beans, salsify, and sliced brussels sprouts, but these green ones have to be very carefully drained or else they are wet and make the omelette sodden.

Of course this omelette is equally useful as a first course for dinner on occasions when one is absolutely sure that dinner can begin twenty minutes after it goes into the oven. It is nasty if it has to be kept warm for more than a minute or two.

HARD-BOILED EGGS WITH TUNNY

Before boiling the eggs, I open a tin of tunny fish in oil, and tip the contents into a strainer over a small bowl and leave it in a cold place until all the oil has dripped into the bowl. Meanwhile I boil the eggs for ten minutes, which is the proper time for setting eggs hard without making them indigestibly tough, according to M. André Simon, who knows all the answers. When the eggs are cold, I shell them and put them into the refrigerator because they are much easier to cut up when they are very cold. Then I make a mayonnaise sauce (see p. 29), using the oil which has drained out of the tin of tunny. Of course, if there is not enough of it, I finish making the sauce with olive oil. The tunny fish is then flaked and mixed with the hard-boiled eggs cut in pieces and with chives or spring onions chopped very small. This mixture is put into a dish

Eggs

and the mayonnaise sauce is poured over it, or else it is put into small separate bowls.

Ovenproof dishes, and small separate pots for eggs, are essential for hot things, but they are dull clumsy objects on a dinner-table. When the course is a cold one, it is surely more attractive if it is dished up in charming china. Little Chinese bowls contain an egg very neatly, and look much nicer than toughened glass or practical pots for the oven.

Fish

When I have cooked fish, I expect it to taste fishy—or, at any rate, to taste of *something*. There are some fish so incurably tasteless that they won't even absorb the flavour of a *court bouillon* or of anything else. Fresh haddock is one of them, and hake another. I would really rather have a perch redolent of river-mud than a hunk of hake like consolidated cotton-wool. Halibut is reasonably fishy, but rather like a mattress in texture. Cod and plaice are better, and turbot better still. Sole is the best of all, except salmon, which I cannot afford. Herrings are excellent, once you have learned how to deal with the bones, and so are mackerel, but they tend to be dry and need stuffing. There are two kinds of cheap fish which do very well as material for messing about with. One is what the fishmongers call rock salmon (for fun, apparently —as its real name is coal-fish). It comes away from its bone, when cooked, in nice solid little fillets, and tastes agreeably of the ocean. Then there is a fish called coley, which you buy in lumpy fillets. It is cheap because people object to its brownish colour. (How odd that the English, who choose brown paint and mud-coloured carpets and porridge-coloured upholstery, insist on having the heart bleached out of their linen and their bread, and even demand chalk-white fish.) The only disadvantage of the off-white coley is that it is a little tough, and must be well cooked.

I wash fish, as soon as I have brought it home, under the cold tap, and scrape off the scales with the back of a knife. (But I try not to let the scales get down the plug-hole—they block up the

Fish

sink faster than anything else.) Fillets I skin, by holding them firmly, skin side upwards, on the draining-board, and lifting the skin with a sharp knife, beginning at the thin end. Mackerel and herrings must be boned, before cooking. The way to do this is, first, to cut off the head. Then grasp the fish firmly by the belly, and make a slit all down the back with a sharp knife. Still holding the fish firmly, press your thumb into the top of the slit until you can feel the backbone, and push your thumb all down one side until you have separated the fish from the bone on that side. Reverse the fish, grasp it tightly again, and do the same thing with your thumb on the other side. The backbone can then be gently extracted with one's thumb and finger, and if you are careful, the fish should still be in one piece, and not in halves. I know this sounds confusing, and so it is, until you get used to doing it. Practise on herrings, and make soup of them if they look very messy. When you have boned the fish, make a slit half-way down the front, and remove all the silvery tubes and little bloody bits which are its guts.

Fish needs to be cooked very slowly and gently or else it will be tough. Whole fish, and some fillets, even if you are going to do other things to them afterwards, are immensely improved by being cooked in a *court bouillon*.

Cold Fish Dishes

FILLETS OF FISH IN ASPIC

I buy the so-called rock-fish for this dish—enough of it to cover completely the bottom of the dish I intend to serve it in. I cook the pieces of fish in a *court bouillon*, drain them, and fillet them. The few, large bones come away very easily, and are put back into the *court bouillon* which is then reduced to a *fumet* (see p. 23). The *fumet* is strained through a cloth, and put in the refrigerator to set. It may have to be made up to a greater quantity by the addition of a little water and a little sherry or cider and a small quantity of gelatine, enough to make it set properly without being a stiff jelly. (If these additions are necessary, the whole amount

Fish

of liquid must of course be heated up and the gelatine stirred into it until it is dissolved, and then strained again.) The cold fish is arranged in a shallow dish, and the chinks between the fillets filled up with pieces of raw diced cucumber and raw (or tinned) diced red pimento, and the gelatinous liquid strained over it. When it has set, finely chopped parsley and chervil are sprinkled over the surface for ornament and flavour.

COLD FILLETS OF SOLE

When I buy the fillets of sole I ask for the bones and trimmings as well. (Many people seem to leave this valuable part of their purchase to be thrown away with the fishmonger's rubbish.) I prepare a *court bouillon*, and while it is simmering I cut up one or two seeded pimentos, and melt them gently in hot oil until they are soft, and then drain them. The fillets of sole are poached in the *court bouillon* for six minutes, and lifted out carefully on a fish-slice so that they drain well, and arranged on a shallow buttered dish. The pieces of cooked pimento are put between them, and then very narrow strips of cold tongue are arranged in a criss-cross pattern over each fillet. Meanwhile, the bones and trimmings of the sole have been put into the *court bouillon*, and it is being reduced to a *fumet*, but not too much reduced—half an hour's cooking is enough. It is then strained and measured, and a white sauce is made with a spoonful of flour and one of butter, and when this *roux* is ready, half a pint of the *fumet* is strained into it gradually, and cooked in a double saucepan until it is thick enough. This quantity will do for four fillets. The sauce is seasoned with salt and black pepper, as required, and a squeeze of lemon juice. (A sauce which is to be served cold needs to be far more highly seasoned than a hot one.) The finished sauce is strained over the fish, and the dish is covered with wet greaseproof paper fastened on with elastic bands and left to get perfectly cold before the paper is removed. Finally the surface of the cold sauce is decorated with slices of lemon cut in quarters and halved stoned olives, arranged in a pattern of some sort.

Fish

COLD FILLETS OF FISH WITH MUSHROOMS

Fillets of cod or plaice, or rock-fish do quite well for this dish, as the mushrooms dominate the flavour, but of course sole is the nicest material of all to use. When I have made a *court bouillon* I poach the fillets in it for six minutes or so—or twelve minutes if they are rock-fish—and drain them and arrange them in a shallow buttered dish. Then I cook half a pound of mushrooms, broken up, in hot oil with a spoonful of lemon juice and a small onion chopped very fine, and some salt and pepper sprinkled over them while they cook. When they are soft, the mushrooms and the *cuisson* are poured into a strainer over the *court bouillon*, so that they are drained and the *cuisson* goes into the pan. The mushrooms are spread over the fish, and the *court bouillon*, with the addition of the fish bones and trimmings, is reduced to a *fumet*, but not very greatly reduced—half an hour's cooking will be enough. Then I make a white *roux* with a spoonful of butter and one of flour, and when it is done I strain into it gradually half a pint of the *fumet*, and flavour it with more salt and pepper as seems necessary and a little lemon juice, and cook it in the double saucepan until it is thick. (This quantity is enough to cover four fillets of fish, and if it is necessary to make a greater quantity, the liquid may be made up with the addition of some cider if there is not enough *fumet*.) The sauce is strained over the fish and mushrooms, and covered with wet greaseproof paper, fastened down, until it is cold. The surface is then decorated with some sort of design which I draw very inefficiently with a skewer dipped in tomato *purée*.

SHRIMPS IN ASPIC

This is a useful dish to make in large quantities for 'fork' luncheons and suppers. I make it in the big meat dishes of an old dinner service, which are just deep enough. I cover the bottom of the dishes completely with peeled cooked shrimps (fresh or tinned), cooked green peas and diced carrots, and diced raw red

Fish

pimento and cucumber and peeled tomato. Some chopped stoned olives are added, and chopped gherkins, and chopped raw chives, and perhaps raw nasturtium seeds and finely chopped raw white endive. The whole thing must make a layer of at least half an inch thick on the dish, and it is of no use to try and make it form a pattern because the aspic will dissarrange it.

I always make a lot of aspic for these dishes, because it is essential to have enough to cover the dishes, and if there is too much it is always useful afterwards for other things. If I have not got enough vegetable *consommé* ready to make it, I use instead a liquid made with a teaspoonful of Marmite perfectly dissolved in three-quarters of a pint of hot water with a clove of crushed garlic heated with it and removed when it is done, and then the liquid is made up to a pint with sherry before the gelatine is dissolved in it. The cooling aspic is poured over the dishes until they are brimming, and they are left in a cool place to set, and then decorated with watercress and nasturtium flowers, or the curly tops of celery.

Hot Fish Dishes

FILLETS OF PLAICE WITH SHALLOTS

For four fillets, I cut ten or a dozen shallots into very thin rings, and put them into an ovenproof dish (which possesses a lid) with two ounces of butter and a chopped clove of garlic. The dish is put, uncovered, into a moderate oven and left until the butter has melted the shallots and they are quite soft. The fillets of plaice, coated with seasoned flour and rolled up and secured with cocktail cherry sticks, are then put in, plenty of salt and pepper are added, and half a pint of white wine or cider. The lid is put on the dish, and it is returned to the oven for ten minutes and then removed. After this preliminary cooking, it can be put in the lower part of a cool oven (300 deg., Gas, No. 2) for half an hour before dinner and will be perfectly cooked with a delicious sauce at the end of that time.

Fish

COLEY AU BLEU

I make a *court bouillon au bleu*—using red wine with the water instead of white wine—and while it cooks I cut up a pound of small white onions and cook them gently in two spoonfuls of oil until they are melted but not really coloured. I put two pounds of coley into a casserole with the onions and their oil, and a clove of crushed garlic and the strained *court bouillon*, with salt and pepper, and cook it with the lid on for two hours in a low oven (300 deg., Gas, No. 2) if at the end of that time I want to have it straight away. If, however, I do all this in advance, I cook it for only one hour; and in this case I put it into the oven at the same heat one hour before I propose to dish it up. It is not an elegant dish, it is simply a good stew of fish and onions in wine.

MOROCCO FILLETS OF FISH

I learned to do this dish in Rabat with small coarse fish, very bony, from a local stream. I now do it with fillets of cod.

I first spread a shallow, buttered dish with enough onion, and tomato, chopped small, to cover the bottom of it. This layer is then sprinkled with chopped parsley and chopped fresh sage. The fillets of fish are laid on this bed, and more chopped parsley and sage are sprinkled over it, and it is then covered and left for an hour or two, while the fish absorbs the flavours. White wine is then poured in until it nearly, but not quite, covers the fish, which is salted and peppered, and then some bits of butter are added, and the fish cooked for forty-five minutes, with grease-proof paper over it, in a moderate oven (350 deg., Gas No. 4). In Morocco the rough, brownish local wine was used. Draught cider is an excellent substitute.

SOLE WITH SOUR CREAM

I skin fillets of sole and rub them with cut lemon and put on each fillet four or five peeled shrimps and a spoonful of very

Fish

finely chopped raw shallot, or chives. I season them with salt and pepper, fold the fillets over so that the stuffing is enclosed, and pack them into a fireproof dish that will just contain them comfortably, having first buttered the dish well. I pour in enough sour cream to cover them, put small bits of butter here and there on the surface, and bake, uncovered, for half an hour in the upper part of a medium hot oven (380 deg., Gas, No. 5). The top ought to be slightly coloured when it is done.

TURBOT IN WHITE WINE

I have the turbot cut in slices an inch thick. They are put in a buttered dish with plenty of chopped onion and chopped skinned tomatoes round them and some of this on top of the slices. Salt and pepper are sprinkled over them, and white wine is poured in to come half-way up the dish. I then add a crushed clove of garlic and try to remember to take it out before anyone gets it on his plate. The dish is covered tightly with greaseproof paper, and baked in a warm oven (330 deg., Gas, No. 3) for forty minutes.

This is equally good hot or cold. If it is to be hot for dinner, it can be prepared two or three hours beforehand with advantage, and left perfectly ready to put into the oven, by which time it will have been marinaded by its dressing.

HALIBUT WITH MUSHROOMS AND BACON

Two pounds of halibut are put into a buttered dish with button mushrooms which have been dipped in melted butter. I break up the fish into biggish pieces with a fork and distribute the mushrooms amongst them. Salt and pepper and the juice of half a lemon are sprinkled over the surface, which is then covered with rashers of bacon. The dish is put uncovered into a moderate oven (340 deg., Gas, No. 3) for forty minutes. Half-way through the cooking, the rashers of bacon are turned over so that the other side of them becomes crisp.

Fish

BAKED FISH

This is a rather solid dish of fish and vegetables, for which I use thick slices of cod, halibut, or turbot. A spoonful of oil is put into a casserole, with a Spanish onion, three cloves of garlic and a stick of celery all chopped small. Two peeled, sliced potatoes and tomatoes are added, well spread about the dish and oiled. The slices of fish are then brushed over with oil and laid on the bed of vegetables, and when they have been salted and peppered well, I cut a lemon into thin slices and lay it all over the fish, and put in a spoonful of tomato *purée* distributed in bits round the edges of the dish. The dish is covered with two layers of greaseproof paper attached firmly, and baked in a moderate oven (340 deg., Gas, No. 3) for forty-five minutes. The lemon is removed before serving.

BURGUNDIAN EELS

Two pounds of eels are cut into slices an inch thick, and the fins snipped off. I make a *court bouillon au bleu* (the wine for which ought to be Burgundy, but can't be, except for extravagant purists) and cook a dozen small shallots in it rather fast, so that the liquid reduces considerably. Then I put in the eel pieces and reduce the heat so that the eel poaches gently for twenty minutes. Meanwhile I prepare a brown *roux*. When the eel is poached, it is removed with a draining-spoon, and the shallots too, and they are put into a buttered casserole. The hot *court bouillon* is strained gradually into the brown *roux* and stirred until it is of the right consistency—a very smooth, thinnish but velvety sauce, highly seasoned with salt and pepper, and a small pinch of nutmeg. It is then poured over the eel and shallots in the casserole, which is immediately covered with wet greaseproof paper to prevent a skin forming on the sauce. This dish is reheated slowly and carefully, in a very low oven (300 deg., Gas, No. 2) for half an hour with the lid on the casserole, and stirred from time to time. A few minutes before serving, some small bits of butter are stirred into it.

Fish

If my (English) guests ask me what it is, I don't tell them that it is eel; it puts them off dreadfully, I find. I tell them that it is a fish dish I had in Burgundy, and then they love it. It is not the cathedral-smell taste of the eel that puts them off, but just the notion of eating something that has wriggled.

BAKED TROUT

This dish cannot be cooked in advance, but it can be prepared, and the cooking is so simple that any willing hand in the kitchen can do what is necessary. I buy one small trout for each person, and put them (gutted, washed and dried) in a buttered fireproof dish, not flat, but standing up on their bellies side by side, and kept in this position by using egg-cups or clean scrubbed potatoes as props round the edges of the dish. They are sprinkled with salt and black pepper and a good deal of chopped parsley, and a lot of butter in small pieces is put on and round them in the dish. Half an hour before they are to be ready, they are put into an oven which has been made fairly hot (400 deg., Gas, No. 6) and after five minutes the heat is reduced by half and the trout are cooked gently for another twenty minutes, being frequently basted with the melted butter in the dish. Then the egg-cups or potatoes are removed and the trout allowed to lie down side by side in the dish, and slices of fresh-cut lemon are arranged on them, and, finally, a pat of *maître d'hôtel* butter is put on each one just before they are brought to the dining-room. (This is butter which has been worked up with salt, pepper, lemon juice, and some very finely chopped parsley. I make it beforehand, shape it into the necessary number of pats, and leave it in the refrigerator.)

MOULES BÉCHAMEL

Mussels ought to be served in the half-shell, but this is too complicated a procedure if they are to be prepared in advance, and so I have them, unshelled, in the sauce. The initial preparation of mussels is a great bore because they have to be washed and scraped in several waters to get rid of their excrescences and sand.

Fish

When the shells are clean, and the last rinsing water contains no sand at all, they are put into a large saucepan with chopped onion and garlic and a *bouquet* and a bit of butter and a little white wine, and cooked and stirred for a few minutes over brisk heat, until they open. They are taken out of the pan as they open and put aside. When they are all out, their *cuisson* is strained through muslin into a pint of Béchamel sauce (see p. 25) which has been made in a double saucepan, and the sauce is cooked and stirred for a little longer, until the added *cuisson* is quite incorporated, and it is really thick. When it is cool, the mussels are put into it. It must be reheated extremely gently, over water which never boils but only simmers, until all is hot enough. It is important to have this done very carefully and slowly, because mussels reheated too fast and too much are liable to be tough, tasteless, and very indigestible. It is a good plan to have the plates for them very hot, rather than warm, and the *moules* Béchamel very warm, rather than hot.

BAKED FISH OMELETTE

This is an omelette of the Spanish variety which makes a very convenient dish for supper after the theatre, with most of the work done in advance and the remaining preparations left ready, as with the Bake Spanish Omelette (see p. 45). I poach a pound of any white fish in a *court bouillon*, drain it, and flake it up in a buttered shallow ovenproof dish. I then chop small a large onion, and break up four ounces of mushrooms, and cook these with a crushed clove of garlic and salt and pepper in a spoonful of oil and a spoonful of the *court bouillon* until they are soft, very slow cooking with frequent stirring. These are then drained and mixed with the fish in the dish, and more salt and pepper are scattered over them, and a little lemon juice, and some chopped parsley. This fish foundation is enough for four (or even five) people. For four, eight eggs and two and a half spoonfuls of cold water are beaten up with a whisk, with several bits of butter, and salt and pepper, and poured over the fish dish which has been getting warm in the oven while the eggs were being beaten. The omelette

Fish

is then left in the oven at a moderate heat (350 deg., Gas, No. 4) for twenty minutes.

FISH REMAINS WITH SCRAMBLED EGGS

The remains of any cooked fish—kippers, haddock, or white fish that has been cooked in a *court bouillon*—can be mixed with scrambled eggs to make an excellent dish, provided that one is generous with the eggs. The flaked fish (completely free from bones) is warmed in a saucepan with a little butter and pepper while the eggs are being scrambled, and then it is all mixed together and served very hot. This, unfortunately, is not a dish that can be cooked ahead—but anyone who is capable of scrambling eggs can do it. Two reliable children will do it beautifully and dish it up on slices of buttered toast—and enjoy every moment of the cooking and the eating.

MACKEREL

I don't understand why mackerel, an oily fish, tends to dry up during cooking, but it does, and needs emollients. If poached in a *court bouillon*, it demands an unctuous sauce such as Hollandaise (see p. 30). If I bake it, I stuff it with a mixture of fat bacon and raw onion and olives, all chopped small and pounded together with salt and pepper. The stuffed fish are put in a buttered dish with a slice of fat bacon laid over each one, the dish is covered with greaseproof paper fastened down, and put in a moderate over (340 deg., Gas, No. 3) for forty minutes. Before serving, the bacon is removed and a little lemon juice sprinkled over the fish. I make a Poulette sauce for it (see p. 27).

HERRINGS IN OATMEAL

This most excellent Scottish standby is not a dish for a dinner-party, but it can be cooked in advance for breakfast, luncheon, or even a supper-party, and is always a success because everyone likes it if the herrings have been properly boned.

Fish

When I have cleaned and boned the herrings I open them out flat, and each one is pressed, front downwards, on a sheet of paper covered with coarse oatmeal seasoned with salt and pepper. The skin side, then uppermost, is painted lightly with oil, and the herring is turned over and pressed again into the oatmeal, so that both sides are coated. It is then put into a frying-pan containing hot oil or lard, and fried for a minute or two on one side, then carefully turned over with the aid of the fish-slice and a palette-knife and fried on the other. When the fish has puffed itself up a little and the oatmeal on both sides is golden, it is lifted out and put on greaseproof paper to drain, skin side down. After I have done all the fish, I collect the remaining browned oatmeal in the pan and deposit it on any bare patches on the herrings.

These herrings can be reheated on a flat buttered dish, uncovered, in a low oven (320 deg., Gas, No. 2) for twenty minutes, and are just as good then as they are when they are first cooked.

STUFFED HERRINGS

The herrings are cleaned and boned, and then stuffed with finely chopped onion, garlic, parsley, and tomato, all mashed up with salt and pepper and a good bit of butter. The skins of the herrings are first brushed with oil, and then as much stuffing as possible is put into each fish, and a cocktail cherry stick is used to fasten it together. I then cook the herrings in a buttered dish, covered with greaseproof paper, in a moderate oven for half an hour (340 deg., Gas, No. 3). They can be eaten either hot or cold; or they can be reheated in a low oven (300 deg., Gas, No. 2) for a quarter of an hour with the addition of a few small bits of butter, which will melt and mingle with the small amount of stuffing that always oozes out of the fish, to make quite a good sauce.

SOUSED HERRINGS

I think soused food is horrible, but I cook it sometimes for people who like it. These herrings are cleaned and boned, painted with oil, and dipped in flour or fine oatmeal which has been

Fish

seasoned with salt and pepper. They are then put in a shallow ovenproof dish, standing on their sides with their tails curled round and fastened to the other end with a cocktail cherry stick. A mixture of chopped onion, garlic, parsley and gherkin is put into the hollow middle of each curled-up herring, and topped with a small spoonful of chutney. Equal parts of vinegar and water are then poured into the dish, to come half-way up the fish, and several cloves and two bay leaves are put into the liquid. The dish is covered with paper, and put into a cool oven (300 deg., Gas, No. 2) for an hour. When cooked and cold, the herrings are taken out, drained on a sieve and then arranged on a dish and decorated with parsley.

KEDGEREE

I like my kedgeree *gras*, like risotto, not dry, like curry rice. The result is unorthodox and oozy.

I make it with a smoked haddock, simmered in water and milk and then drained and flaked. I melt three-quarters of a pound of unpolished rice in a spoonful of hot bacon fat, stirring all the time until the fat is absorbed, and then put in the fish *cuisson* and cook the rice in this, stirring frequently and adding more hot water if necessary until the rice is cooked. The pot is then covered with a thick absorbent cloth and stood in a warm place for half an hour, so that the cloth may absorb the steam and the rice will dry. The flaked haddock is mixed with the rice very thoroughly with two forks until there is no visible fish, only a general impression of fish-whiskers adhering to every grain of rice. A hard-boiled egg and a good bit of parsley, both chopped very small, are mixed into the kedgeree then. It is put into a buttered ovenproof dish with a lid, and bits of bacon fat are dotted about on the surface. It is heated with the lid on, in a low oven (300 deg., Gas, No. 2) for half an hour.

KIPPER KEDGEREE

Two kippers are enough for three-quarters of a pound of rice. I pour boiling water on the kippers and leave them in it for five

Fish

minutes. (It seems to me a terrible waste of time and utensils to cook them in any other way.) Then I drain them and remove the flesh from the bones and flake it. The rice is cooked as in the last recipe, using plain hot water, as the kipper-water is simply a dye-bath and must be thrown away. When mixing the flaked kipper with the rice, I sprinkle in a teaspoonful of dry mustard. The kedgeree is then finished with hard-boiled egg and parsley, and reheated when required.

PINK KEDGEREE

This is the same as the kedgeree in the first recipe, except that when cooking the rice I put in, after the first addition of liquid, three large, skinned tomatoes, chopped small, and stir them well into the rice as it cooks. At the end, instead of parsley, I put in a spoonful of celery chopped finely.

If intended for luncheon or supper, all of these kedgerees are greatly improved by the addition of finely chopped onion or chives cooked with the rice in the bacon fat at the beginning, and I like a clove of garlic as well. But of course these additions are unacceptable to the Briton's breakfast palate.

FISH CAKES

I make these with the remains of any kedgeree, adding some stiffish mashed potato, or else some fresh white bread-crumbs, and squeezing it all together into solid flat cakes. These are brushed over with egg, coated with fine dry bread-crumbs, and fried in hot fat until they are evenly coloured all over, then drained on greaseproof paper. They may be reheated quite successfully on a flat uncovered dish in a low oven (320 deg., Gas, No. 2) for twenty minutes.

REMAINS OF KEDGEREE

Kedgeree, mixed with a little Béchamel or tomato sauce, can be put into buttered scallop shells, covered with fresh bread-

Fish

crumbs and little bits of butter, and baked in a moderate oven (360 deg., Gas, No. 4) for twenty minutes—useful first course to leave prepared for supper after the theatre, as it can be put into the oven the moment after one's return.

The remains of kedgeree, like the remains of all rice dishes, can be used to stuff things with, such as tomatoes, marrows, and green peppers, hot—and rolled-up slices of ham or garlic sausage, cold, for a cold first course. In either case it can be diversified by the addition of chopped raw chives or olives or cheese, or cooked sultanas or raisins, and improved by being bound with a little white sauce.

Pasta

British dishes of spaghetti and macaroni are often so dull and tasteless that the more enterprising eaters in our Islands have come to regard the stuff with contempt except when they cross the Channel. This is really rather a pity, because it can easily be made delicious, and it has the advantages of being cheap, digestible, and certain to take the edge off the most ferocious adolescent appetite. When I think about pasta, I dismiss from my mind the slimy stodge called macaroni cheese on the table d'hôte menu of seaside hotels, sorrowfully swallowed on Sunday evenings as the cold rain drove in from the sea and the great grey waves broke over the Marine Parade—and I try even harder to forget the terrible substance that the Ministry of Food called soyaghetti in the days of the war, and which was encountered in the form of haunting puddings. Instead, I conjure up a picture of a *trattoria* in Naples, full of joyous Wops reeking of garlic, who are tucking into tagliatelli with terrific gusto and a total disregard of Torquay table manners. (Of course the Italians do add to their own difficulties by leaving the long pasta unbroken in the cooking, and coiling it wildly round their forks before hurling it into their mouths. I see no point in this, since almost all the pasta here is bought prefabricated and can be broken up into manageable lengths before it is cooked. The English are by nature adroit eaters. They can even manage chopsticks if they must—but it is unreasonable to expect them to wrap a twelve-inch length of foreign food round a fork while talking really well about a Test

Pasta

Match or the income tax. They can do it, of course, but only with damnable difficulty, and the sparkling conversation suffers. So I break the pasta up before I cook it. It tastes just the same.)

SPAGHETTI WITH TOMATOES

Four ounces of fat bacon rashers are cut into pieces and cooked with a chopped onion and two cloves of garlic in a big saucepan until the fat has come out of the bacon and coloured the onion very slightly. Then four large, skinned chopped tomatoes are put in, and stirred for a minute or two, after which enough hot water is added to accommodate the spaghetti, with salt, black pepper, and a *bouquet garni*. When the water boils fast, the spaghetti is put in, broken into short lengths, and the water is kept boiling fairly fast during the cooking, for the spaghetti must circulate briskly. It is stirred from time to time to ensure that none of it sticks to the saucepan. When the spaghetti is thoroughly cooked—it will take about twenty minutes—the liquid is drained away (and kept for soup material) and the well-drained pasta is put into a hot buttered casserole with plenty of chopped parsley and several bits of butter, and thoroughly stirred and mixed. The covered casserole may be left for half an hour or forty minutes at the bottom of a low oven and the contents will take no harm. However, if it must be cooked even further ahead of the time it is wanted, it is better to defer the addition of parsley and butter until it is warming in a colander over hot water in a saucepan on gentle heat. Butter and parsley should be stirred in at the last minute before serving the dish.

TAGLIATELLI

This is the one variety of pasta that cannot be bought prefabricated in packets. Of course it is far more trouble to make it than it is to buy it in a packet, but it is an interesting culinary exercise, and the result is delicious. This is the basic pasta recipe, always used before the stuff was made in factories, and still in use all over Italy, and in a few Italian restaurants in England.

Pasta

A pound of plain flour is put into a big basin, a hole is made in the middle of the flour, and four eggs and a teacupful of warm salted water (already lightly mixed together in a jug) are stirred into it with a wooden spoon, gradually, beating with the spoon when all is combined. Then the paste is kneaded thoroughly and rolled out to the thickness of about an eighth of an inch. Each thin sheet of paste is spread on a clean cloth for half an hour, to dry, and afterwards cut into strips of a quarter of an inch wide. Meanwhile a big pot full of veal broth is brought to the boil, and the tagliatelli put into it and kept briskly boiling until they are cooked. This will take about twenty minutes, but I always make sure by taking out a little bit and eating it—pasta that tastes slightly uncooked is horrid. The tagliatelli are drained well, and mixed with plenty of hot fresh tomato sauce (see p. 31). If they are made in advance, they can be reheated in a colander over a saucepan of hot water until they are really hot, and the hot tomato sauce mixed with them then.

TAGLIATELLI VERDI

These are made in the same way as the white tagliatelli, except that a handful of spinach or watercress is cooked in boiling water for five minutes, drained, and pressed through a wire sieve into the mixture of eggs and salted water in the jug. This gives the pasta its green colour and different flavour. It is dressed with a sauce made of four ounces of butter and one ounce of flour, stirred together with salt and pepper in a double saucepan until it is cooked and very smooth. This very simple and mildly flavoured dish depends upon its rich texture to please the palates of people who expect pasta to be slimy and stiff.

MACARONI AND STEAK

This is an ample dish for eight, or even ten, hungry people. I put two pounds of cheap 'stewing' steak in a marinade overnight, and then drain it. Two spoonfuls of oil are then heated in a big pan, and two Spanish onions, two cloves of garlic, two carrots, a turnip,

Pasta

and a small parsnip, all chopped small, are cooked in the oil until they are melted but not brown. The steak, rolled in seasoned flour, is then cooked with the vegetables until it is sealed. Enough hot vegetable stock is poured into the saucepan to cover everything, salt and pepper and a *bouquet garni* are added, and it is brought gently to the boil and simmered very slowly for two hours. The liquid is then drained off, and when the meat is cold it is chopped into very small pieces. The *cuisson* is not skimmed of its fat, but heated up with the strained marinade, and enough hot water added to make about a quart of liquid. When it boils, it is seasoned with salt and lemon juice and pepper if these are required, and then a pound of macaroni broken into very short lengths is put in by degrees (so that the liquid never stops boiling) and kept moving briskly in the saucepan until it is cooked. It takes longer than spaghetti—about half an hour. It is then drained, and mixed thoroughly with the chopped meat. I make a large brown *roux* in a double saucepan with two spoonfuls of butter and two of flour, and when it is ready I make a sauce by adding gradually a pint of the strained *cuisson*, hot, adding, at the end, a teaspoonful of made mustard and a spoonful of port. When the sauce is thick enough, it is strained over the meat and macaroni and stirred into it thoroughly. The mixture is turned into a large ovenproof dish, and the surface is first lightly sprinkled with chopped parsley, and then thickly with grated cheese, and a few small bits of butter are put on it. It is reheated in the upper part of a moderate oven (340 deg., Gas, No. 3) for half an hour.

SPAGHETTI WITH MEAT SAUCE

I always make this when I have the residue of something excellent in a casserole, jellified remains containing scraps of meat or bird, and vegetables, all covered with a layer of cold fat. I remove the fat with a spoon and put it into a saucepan and put into it about a pint and a half of hot water, season it with salt and pepper and a *bouquet garni* and the juice of half a lemon, and bring it to the boil. Then I put in half a pound of spaghetti, broken into short lengths, and let it boil quite fast until the spaghetti is cooked,

Pasta

stirring occasionally to ensure that it does not stick to the pan. Meanwhile the casserole containing the remains has been put into the bottom of a low oven to get warm and melt the jelly. When the spaghetti is cooked, it is drained, and then put into the casserole and well stirred up so that the melted residue is distributed throughout it as a meat sauce. If the original dish was a good one, this one will be good too.

GNOCCHI

I have tried four or five ways of making gnocchi, and this one is the best, in my opinion. I put four ounces of butter and a pint of milk with a crushed clove of garlic in a saucepan with salt and pepper, and stir them together over gentle heat until the butter is quite melted and mixed with the milk, and when the milk comes to the boil I sprinkle into it four ounces of semolina. This has to be done gradually but still fairly fast, and must be stirred firmly and continuously to prevent any lumps forming while the mixture thickens. As soon as the mixture is solid enough to leave the sides of the pan, it is taken off the stove and allowed to cool, and then put in large rough heaps, separate, in a buttered shallow ovenproof dish. The clove of garlic is removed, and chopped parsley is scattered over the gnocchi. I then make a pint of Béchamel sauce and stir four spoonfuls of grated cheese into it when it is nearly cooked and go on stirring for a few minutes longer. This sauce is poured over the gnocchi, reheated, and if the dish is to be served at once, it is put for a minute or two under the grill until the sauce begins to brown. If, however, it is cooked ahead of the time it is wanted, it can be reheated most successfully in the upper part of a moderate oven (350 deg., Gas, No. 4) uncovered, for half an hour. It should be bubbling and just coloured on top when it is taken out.

GNOCCHI WITH BACON AND MUSHROOMS

I make the gnocchi and put it in spoonfuls in a shallow buttered dish and let it cool. Button mushrooms are cooked in a little bacon

Pasta

fat and a spoonful of white wine, and when soft they are distributed among the gnocchi, and their *cuisson* poured over them. Then rashers of bacon are laid over it all, and the dish put in the upper part of a moderate oven (350 deg., Gas, No. 4) for half an hour, but after a quarter of an hour the bacon is turned over so that the other sides of the rashers are crisped.

TOMATO AND CHEESE GNOCCHI

This gnocchi is made with a pint of tomato soup (see p. 32) and a little cream, instead of with milk. When it is cooked, it is poured while still hot into a buttered ovenproof dish and allowed to cool in a mass instead of being divided into pieces. When cold, the surface is covered with bits of butter and plenty of grated cheese. The dish is reheated in a brisk oven (400 deg., Gas, No. 6) for twenty minutes, or until the cheese is bubbling with the butter.

GNOCCHI WITH VEGETABLES

Two spoonfuls of oil or bacon fat are made hot in a strong saucepan, and a chopped Spanish onion and a chopped clove of garlic are cooked in it until they are melted; then a piece of chopped turnip and a chopped stick of celery are added; then an apple and two tomatoes, both peeled and cut up. All these are stirred together, with salt and pepper, until they are a soft mass. Four spoonfuls of semolina are then put in by degrees, and stirred carefully into the mixture until it is thick and ready to leave the sides of the pan. About three-quarters of a pint of any hot vegetable *cuisson* are then poured in gradually, and stirred until there are no semolina lumps, and then the heat is reduced to the minimum and the mixture left to simmer until it is thick enough to leave the sides of the pot again. It must be stirred from time to time to prevent it sticking. When done, it is turned at once into a buttered ovenproof dish. The top, when cold, is thickly sprinkled with grated cheese and bits of butter are added, and it is reheated in a brisk oven (400 deg., Gas, No. 6) until the cheese is bubbling and browning a little.

Pasta

GNOCCHI WITH FISH

This is a substantial main dish for a maigre dinner. I make gnocchi with milk as in the first recipe, and put it in spoonfuls in a really ample buttered ovenproof dish. A pound and a half of any white fish is cooked in a *court bouillon*, drained and flaked. Four ounces of mushrooms, broken up, are cooked in a little butter and a spoonful of the *court bouillon* until they are soft, and then mixed with the fish. Two hard-boiled eggs are cut up and added to this mixture, which is then spread round the gnocchi in the big dish, and the cheese sauce (Béchamel, with grated cheese added at the end of the cooking) is poured over it. It is reheated for twenty minutes in a moderate oven (360 deg., Gas, No. 4) for twenty minutes, and then put for a minute under the grill to colour the surface of the sauce.

The remains of any pasta can be used to combine with chopped meat, game, or vegetables for stuffing peppers, marrows, and tomatoes. Small quantities of it can be used to diversify vegetable soups.

Rice

I use only unpolished Patna rice, and before cooking it I wash it well in a wire sieve under the cold tap in order to get rid of any loose starchy coating of the grains which makes them sticky in cooking. It is then drained well, spread out on a big sieve so that all the water drips out.

RISOTTO NOËL

I make this dish every year in vast quantities for a Christmas-party fork-supper, and almost every year I think of some new addition to increase the interest and to swell the bulk of this 'house dish'. Most of the ingredients are cheap ones—an important consideration when so much of it has to be made—and the few expensive items are justified by the resulting variety of tidbits discovered when eating it, and by the fine, confused flavour produced. I make it in batches of two pounds of rice, for which I give the recipe which follows. This quantity is enough for eight or ten people.

Before starting to cook the risotto, I assemble the following things: four ounces of scrap bacon rashers; six ounces of fresh pork; six ounces of lean, cooked ham; half a pound of mushrooms; three pimentos; eight ounces of grated cheese; eight ounces of chopped carrots; four chopped Spanish onions; two ounces of green olives; a small tin of tunny fish; a small tin of crab; two handfuls of raisins; two ounces of chicken

Rice

livers; a cupful of chopped parsley; and a potful of vegetable stock.

The vegetable stock is extremely highly flavoured. It is made of the *cuisson* of the carrots, added to the *cuisson* of any other vegetable which I happen to have cooked the day before. I open the tin of crab and drain its liquid into the stock. I cook the mushrooms very gently in a little butter and two spoonfuls of the stock, take them out when they are soft and put in the seeded, chopped peppers, with a little more butter and one more spoonful of stock and cook them until they are soft, then drain them. The raisins, washed, are then simmered for a few minutes in the same liquid, and drained. The liquid is then put into the pot of stock, and the chicken livers are *sauté* very gently in butter, and drained when they are done, and the liquid buttered juice that remains goes into the stock. This pot of vegetable stock has now acquired a variety of flavours, and is rather greasy, which does not matter because the risotto is a *gras* dish and can take any amount of fat—and fat holds flavours far better than any *cuisson dégraissé*. The stock is heated, tasted, and more salt and pepper added, and a pinch of nutmeg and a teaspoonful of grated root ginger, until it tastes almost intolerably highly seasoned. This is what is wanted, because it is going to be absorbed by unseasoned rice. It must be very salt, and very spicy and 'hot'.

When this is done, I start to cook the risotto. I chop up the bacon and the pork and put them in a very large saucepan over a fair heat, moving them about occasionally with a spoon, until they are becoming crisp and frizzled. While this is going on, I have opened the tin of tunny and drained the contents of it, keeping the oil, and flaking up the fish with a fork. Then, when the big pan is well provided with the fat which has come out of the pork and bacon, I put the finely chopped onions into it, and let them melt and become a light yellow colour over moderate heat. (It is important to chop them small, because long shreds of cooked onion are inconvenient things to encounter in a dish which must be eaten with a fork.) When the onions are just coloured, I put in the oil which has been drained from the tin of tunny fish, and wait for a minute or two to let it get hot, and then I put in the two

Rice

pounds of rice, and stir it about to ensure that it is well oiled all over. It is kept cooking in the hot fat with the onions, and two very finely chopped cloves of garlic which are put in at this stage, for about five minutes, and prevented from sticking to the bottom of the pot by frequent scrapes with a wooden spoon. In the intervals of doing this, I prepare an extra large *bouquet garni*, with twice the contents of the ordinary one. Then, when the rice has evidently absorbed the fat and it is just beginning to change colour, some of the hot vegetable stock is poured on to it, and it is stirred again and the bottom of the pot scraped free of any adhering grains. The *bouquet garni* is put in as the rice simmers until the first addition of stock has been absorbed, and more is then added, and stirred in and absorbed, until the rice is perfectly cooked but still retains the grains individually and not amalgamated, and the latest addition of liquid has been taken up entirely, so that the risotto is not sloppy, but consolidated. Then I take the pot off the heat and stand it at the back of the stove, covered with a thick cloth to absorb the steam, for about ten minutes. At the end of this time I mix into it, with a fork, the grated cheese. (Parmesan is best, but very expensive. I use the remains of bits of hard English cheese which have become dry and even harder in the refrigerator.) When the cheese is thoroughly incorporated, the risotto is turned into a large bowl, to give plenty of room in which to stir while mixing with it the ham (chopped small), the chicken livers, pimentos, carrots, olives, and crab, all chopped small, the flaked tunny, the raisins, and the chopped parsley, and chopped mushrooms. While doing this mixing, I scatter a drift of celery salt and a grind of pepper over it as I stir and mix, at each major turnover of the mass of rice. By the time it is all mixed, the risotto is alarmingly stiff, and feels as if it were about to set like cement. However, it is then put into a buttered earthenware pot and left thankfully in the larder until the next evening. Then it is put into a very low oven (290 deg., Gas, No. 1) for three-quarters of an hour, with greaseproof paper over it instead of its lid, and when it comes to be eaten it is as agreeably soft and unctuous as I could wish, and moreover it is a pleasant source of surprise and interest to anyone who considers what is on his plate.

Rice

RISOTTO MILANESE

Plenty of good veal broth (see p. 36) is necessary to make this risotto. The broth (which has been cooled and degreased beforehand) is heated up in readiness for the cooking, and a little of it is put into a cup with a good pinch of saffron, which is left to soak in it.

Two spoonfuls of oil are made hot in a saucepan, and half a pound of rice, washed and well drained, is stirred in it until the oil is absorbed. Then four ounces of mushrooms, broken up into small pieces, are put in, and some of the veal broth, and after stirring for a minute or two I taste it at this stage and add as much more salt and pepper as seems necessary—or even more, because rice, like potato, seems to reduce the strength of seasoning as it cooks. Then the soaked saffron is added, and more broth, a little at a time, stirring constantly, until the rice is exactly cooked—soft, but unbroken, and not at all sloppy. It is then removed from the heat and put to stand in a warm place at the back of the stove with a thick cloth over the pot to absorb the steam which rises from it. When it is thoroughly evaporated it should be light and slightly fluffy.

This risotto is best when eaten at once, and not reheated. It takes a good twenty minutes to evaporate completely, and comes to no harm if left in the cloth-covered pot for as long as half an hour before being dished up. However, it is still a good dish if it has to be reheated, which should be done in a buttered bowl covered with greaseproof paper over a saucepan of hot, not boiling, water for half an hour.

Some people detest the taste of saffron. I don't give this risotto to people whose tastes are unknown to me, ever since a candid friend ate one mouthful of it and exclaimed: 'This stuff tastes like medicine!'

PRAWN RISOTTO

I make this when I have a *court bouillon* left after cooking fish. The *court bouillon* is strained, and heated in readiness.

Rice

Two dozen shelled prawns are cooked gently in butter in a big pan, and then removed and kept warm. A little more butter is added to what is in the pan, and a finely chopped onion, and when the onion is melted but not coloured, a pound of washed and well-drained rice is put in, and stirred until it has absorbed the butter. Then some of the hot *court bouillon* is added, and a little more salt—other additional seasoning ought not to be needed if the *court bouillon* was properly made. The rice is stirred constantly, and more of the hot liquid added in small quantities until the rice is cooked—soft but unbroken—and all of the last addition of liquid has been taken up in it. Then two spoonfuls of chopped parsley are stirred into it, and it is removed from the heat, the pan covered with a thick cloth to absorb the steam, and it is left to evaporate in a warm place, preferably at the back of the stove while other cooking goes on. When it has dried, it is stirred and loosened with two forks—rice cooked with butter is delicious, but tends to be sticky—and the prawns are gently mixed with it. It is best eaten at once, but can be reheated in a buttered bowl covered with greased paper over hot, not boiling, water.

COLD RISOTTO

This is a good dish to make in large quantities for a fork supper in the summer, or, in the quantities given in this recipe, for the last course at a summer dinner-party for six. In the latter case, I dish it up surrounded with watercress.

A saucepanful of vegetable *cuisson*, highly flavoured with salt, pepper, lemon juice, chervil, and a pinch of ground root ginger, is needed. Strong flavouring is necessary because rice served cold tends to taste of nothing, unless the seasoning has been emphatic when it was cooked.

Four ounces of fat rashers of bacon are cut into pieces and cooked in a strong saucepan until they are just beginning to get crisp, and most of the fat has come out. Then a finely chopped onion and clove of garlic are put in, and cooked with the bacon until faintly coloured. Half a pound of rice, washed and well drained, is then stirred into the bacon and onion until all the fat

Rice

has been absorbed, and then hot vegetable stock is added, by degrees, to cook the rice, which must be stirred all the time, and is done when it is soft but not broken, and all the liquid in the pan has been absorbed. It is then left in a warm place to evaporate with a thick cloth over the pan.

Four ounces of mushrooms, broken up, are cooked in a bit of butter and a spoonful of stock, very gently, until they are soft, then removed and left to cool. A handful of washed sultanas is then cooked in the mushroom *cuisson* until they are soft and fat, when they are drained and cooled. Meanwhile, I chop up four ounces of lean ham, one large seeded pimento, three inches of peeled cucumber, a handful of chives or spring onions, and plenty of parsley. When the cooked things are cold, everything is mixed together carefully with two forks, so that all the additions are distributed throughout the rice without breaking up the grains. This dish is kept in the refrigerator, or in the coolest place available, until it is wanted.

SAVE-ALL RISOTTO

Instincts of frugality drove me to devise this dish. I hate throwing away anything edible, but the bits of fat trimmed off breasts of mutton and chops and cutlets are so daunting that even the dog sniffs and turns away. But they are the 'gags' that sustained life in the little Charles Lamb, and who am I to scorn them? So I accommodate them in a dish of rice, which is rather agreeably flavoured, and is a heartening sort of stodge. It is uncommonly indigestible.

About two handfuls of mutton fat chopped small are put into a strong saucepan, and when the fat begins to run, a Spanish onion and a clove of garlic chopped very finely are added. Two or three minutes later, a small turnip cut into thin slices is put in, and then a peeled, chopped apple and tomato. All these are cooked together, and stirred until they are beginning to colour and coagulate, and then half a pound of washed and drained rice is added, and stirred until it has taken up all the fat. This must be done over lowered heat, and takes longer than it would if cooked

Rice

in oil or butter, as the mutton goes on rendering its fat during this stage of the cooking, and constant stirring is essential. Salt and pepper are sprinkled in by degrees, and the rice is simmered until it is soft and thick and no longer sloppy. A sprinkling of caraway seeds is added towards the end of the cooking, and the juice of half an orange, and the mass is stirred firmly until it is solid—too solid to benefit from the evaporation process which I use to finish all other risottos. It can be eaten straight away, or else reheated in a battered casserole with the lid on for half an hour in a very low oven (300 deg., Gas, No. $1\frac{1}{2}$).

Remains of risotto can be used in many ways. It can be made into stuffing for pimentos, marrows, aubergines, tomatoes, and cucumbers. It can be mixed with a little flaked cooked fish left from another dish, and a spoonful or two of thick sauce, and put into shells or a pie dish, covered with bread-crumbs and bits of butter, and baked gently. It can be mashed with left-over vegetables and a little sauce, and heated and spread on hot buttered toast as a savoury. It can be stirred into hot vegetable stock to make soup. It can even be mashed with minced meat to make rissoles—but not by me.

Birds

The awkward thing about a chicken is that two people have got to have the legs. This may give rise to a faint feeling of resentment in the leg-eaters' hearts—dating, no doubt, from childhood days, when elders and betters naturally cornered the 'white meat' —and, no matter how perfectly cooked the legs may be, there will be two people who feel that they have not had a very good dinner. The only answer to this difficulty is to cook two chickens for a dinner-party of six or eight people, and to use up all the legs afterwards in a pie or a 'made dish'. This is not a very great extravagance, because the four legs and all the odd bits on two chicken carcasses provide quite a lot of material which can be made into another substantial and excellent dish, for six people. A pair of fowls can thus be dressed to feed twelve people, which is economical enough in all conscience. Moreover dowager hens can be made delicious by artful cooking, and the cost of an ample dowager, by the pound, is much less than that of a stringy young bird. I would always rather give each guest the white meat of a carefully cooked and dressed boiling fowl, than see two of them looking resignedly at the drumsticks of a roast cockerel.

STEWED FOWL IN WINE

I get a large boiling fowl for this dish, and use a saucepan big enough to contain it with ease. Four ounces of fat scrap bacon are put into the saucepan over a low heat, and when plenty of

Birds

fat has come out of them, a Spanish onion chopped small and a chopped clove of garlic are added and cooked until they are slightly coloured. Then the trussed fowl is put in, and browned all over. I then pour in half a pint of red wine and add enough hot water to come half-way up the bird, salt, pepper and a *bouquet garni*, and four ounces of mushrooms broken in pieces. The liquid is brought slowly to the boil, skimmed, and then left to simmer very gently for two and a half hours. It is important that the lid of the pot should fit tightly, so that almost no steam escapes. When the chicken is removed, I fish out the pieces of mushroom with a draining-spoon, and then let the *cuisson* simmer with the lid off for about three-quarters of an hour, by which time it should be reduced by half, and it is then strained into a bowl. When it is perfectly cold, the fat is removed from the surface of the stock, which should have set in a jelly.

If I propose to have the chicken as a hot dish, I carve it and arrange the pieces in an ovenproof dish with the mushrooms and the bits of onion, and put the jelly into the dish as well, cover it all with two layers of greaseproof paper well secured, and reheat it in a low oven (320 deg., Gas, No. 2) for half an hour.

If the dish is to be a cold one, the jellied stock is warmed again after the fat has been removed, and then strained through a cloth to make it clear, after which it is put into the refrigerator until it is firmly set. The chicken is carved, the skin removed, and it is arranged in a large shallow dish. Two or three spoonfuls of the jelly are then put in a bowl over hot water, and when the jelly is somewhat melted, I mask the pieces of chicken with it, using a spoon, and a palette-knife to spread it on. The rest of the jelly, when firm, is chopped and put round the edges of the dish, and decorated with sprigs of watercress and scraps of red pimento.

CHICKEN PIE

This is made with a boiled fowl, cooked as in the recipe for Stewed Fowl, only white wine may be used instead of red, or even cider. (Or, if I have cooked two fowls and have four legs left, the pie is made with the meat from the legs, and all the scraps that

Birds

can be cut off the carcass. When everything visible has been cut off, I turn the carcass upside down, where there is a surprisingly good field for further slicing with a small, sharp knife.)

The carcass is made into a really strong broth first. It is broken up, and the pieces browned in hot oil with an onion, carrot, turnip, stick of celery, and clove of garlic, all chopped. Hot water is poured in to cover all of it, a *bouquet garni* and salt and pepper added, and the pot kept at simmering point for three hours. Drained and cold, this broth is skimmed of its fat, and ought to have jellified.

A quarter of a pound of mushrooms are cooked in a little butter and a spoonful of the broth until they are soft, and then drained. A handful of raisins is simmered in some of the broth, and drained too. Three eggs are boiled for ten minutes, cooled and shelled. I then grease a pie dish, and chop the chicken, eggs and mushrooms, and also two or three slices of lean ham, and mix them all with the raisins and a spoonful of chopped parsley in the pie dish, sprinkling the mixture with salt and pepper and a little nutmeg. Enough melted broth is poured into the dish to come within half an inch of the top of it. An egg-cup is put in the middle to hold up the paste (or, if the egg-cup is the wrong height, a tall potted-meat jar, or a short Elizabeth Arden one).

I make the pastry with half a pound of plain flour and three ounces of butter and three of lard, with a teaspoonful of salt and the juice of half a lemon and just enough cold water to make a manageable dough that leaves the fingers dry. The dough is rolled out into an oblong, folded in three, and this is done twice more before putting it into the larder with a damp cloth over it for an hour. Then I roll it out to the thickness of half an inch, draw upon it the pattern of the pie dish with the point of a sharp knife, and then draw the line of an outer oval an inch larger. This outer circle of paste is then cut off and put on the wetted rim of the pie dish, the overhanging edges are trimmed off with scissors, and dents are made in it all round, with the back of a knife. ('Knocking-up', this is called—a rather poetic term of art in English cookery.) I brush this pastry edging on top with cold water, and put on the main oval pieces of paste, pressing down the edge with

Birds

the back of a knife on to the border already in place, and making another set of dents all round the pie. With the remaining scraps of paste, I make four leaf-shaped pieces and arrange them in the middle for ornament. The whole surface is then brushed over with beaten egg, and I make a hole with a skewer near the middle to let the steam out—but not bang over the egg-cup, of course. The pie is then baked in an oven which has been heated already for ten minutes and is fairly hot (430 deg., Gas, No. 7) until the pastry is just the right colour. (As the contents have been cooked already, there is no need to lower the heat and ensure that they are cooked before the crust is too dark, which has to be done if the pie's contents are raw.) If the pie is to be served hot, it will come to no harm if left for twenty minutes or so in the bottom of a very cool oven after it has finished cooking. It is a very good cold pie.

VOL-AU-VENT LATOUR

The chicken filling for this *vol-au-vent* is made with the breast (not the legs) of a fowl cooked in wine as described in the recipe for Stewed Fowl (see p. 77).

The puff pastry for the *vol-au-vent* case is made with half a pound of plain white flour and half a pound of butter. The flour is sieved into a bowl with a teaspoonful of salt, and one ounce of the butter is rubbed into it. Then a hollow is made in the mixture, and the juice of half a lemon is put into it, and enough water to make a stiff paste, which is kneaded quickly and thoroughly until it is not sticky, when it is left, in a lump, in a cold place for a few minutes. I then roll it out into an oblong shape with square corners, half an inch thick. The butter has been squeezed in a clean dry cloth until it is a flat oblong shape, and any moisture that exudes from it has been absorbed in the cloth. This thin oblong pat of butter is put across the middle of the paste, and the two end sections are folded over it, the edges are pressed down, and the paste put in the cold place again for a quarter of an hour. Then it is rolled out again to the original size and shape, folded in three, edges pressed down, and returned to the cold place (larder, or refrigerator). All this has to be done twice more, making alto-

Birds

gether three resting periods for the air to expand in the paste, which should be covered with a clean damp cloth while it is resting. Finally, it is rolled out into an oval of about an inch and a quarter thick, and tidy in shape. With the point of a sharp knife, a cut is made all round the oval, an inch inside the edge—but this cut must not go through the paste, it is intended only to be a light incision to mark the lid of the *vol-au-vent*. The surface of the paste is then brushed over with beaten egg—but on no account must the thick sides be brushed, as that would stop them rising.

The oven has been heated for ten minutes to the right heat (450 deg., Gas, No. 8) before the *vol-au-vent* is put in, on a greased, floured baking-tin, and baked for about half an hour. I look at it from time to time, and when it seems to have risen to the proper height, I lower the heat a little and wait until it is attractively coloured. Then, while it is still hot, I scoop out the lid (indicated by the cut in the pastry) with a spoon, and most of the soft paste inside the *vol-au-vent*, but I take care to leave a good thick layer of paste at the bottom. The underneath of the lid is carefully pared of surplus paste, and these two pieces of pastry are put in the larder.

For the filling, I cook gently in butter a quarter of a pound of mushrooms, and then drain them while a handful of peeled shrimps is cooking gently in the same butter. I chop four ounces of cold, cooked breast of chicken, a dozen stoned French olives, the mushrooms, and a handful of parsley, and mix them with the shrimps. Then I make a sauce with a spoonful of butter and one of flour, and, when the *roux* is cooked, half a pint of degreased chicken broth. The chopped mixture is stirred into the sauce, and it is left ready to fill the *vol-au-vent* case. I do this only just before I want it, and when the filling is in, the lid is put on the *vol-au-vent*, and it is heated on a greased and floured baking-tin for twenty minutes in a cool oven (310 deg., Gas, No. 2).

It is certainly a major culinary undertaking to produce this excellent dish. It is fascinating work, but it takes up a lot of time and needs undivided attention—it would be hard to make a good *vol-au-vent* while amusing a small child and laundering the loose covers or pondering the possibilities of arranging Handley Cross

Birds

for television. Fortunately, any competent baker will take an order for a *vol-au-vent* case, and in my experience his product is always more shapely than mine, and very nearly as light and buttery in every flake. Then there is nothing to do except to prepare the filling, and to reheat the whole thing.

BOUCHÉES LATOUR

Instead of making a *vol-au-vent*, I sometimes make small *bouchée* cases out of the paste treated in the same way, and use a wineglass as a pattern for them when cutting the paste. They take a little less time to bake, and I have to watch them carefully while they rise, and colour. Their little lids are removed with a teaspoon, and some of their interiors carefully scooped out. The filling is the same as for the *vol-au-vent*, except that everything is chopped smaller, and rather less of it is required. These *bouchées* are equally good hot, or cold, as a first course. The obliging baker will take an order for the pastry *bouchée* cases at a pinch.

(To use up the remains of the pastry after the *bouchées* have been cut out, I cut it up into little triangles and squares and strips, roll them in sugar and caraway seeds, and bake them at the same time, and use them, when cold, as a garnish for an apple meringue or a *purée* of apricots.)

CHICKEN SHEPHERD'S PIE

This is a simple and satisfactory way of using up the remains of a cooked chicken. Having cut off every scrap of meat from the carcass, I make a strong broth of the broken bones, browning them first with an onion in hot fat. When the broth is cold and has been degreased, I make a sauce with half a pint of it and a brown *roux*, and season it highly with salt, pepper, nutmeg and a squeeze of lemon juice. I chop two large onions and melt them in a spoonful of oil, remove them and cook in the same oil four ounces of mushrooms, and a seeded, chopped pimento. (Failing pimento, I substitute two sticks of celery or a piece of celeriac, chopped very small.) The cooked vegetables, well drained, are mixed with

Birds

the chopped chicken and the sauce (which should have been reduced to a thick consistency) and put into a buttered pie dish. This is covered with a half-inch layer of *purée* potatoes (see p. 122) and if I use the remains of *purée* potatoes cooked the day before, I warm them in a colander over hot water to make them malleable. The pie is baked in a moderate oven (360 deg., Gas, No. 4) for about half an hour—until the potato is just coloured and crisp on top.

GOOSE SHEPHERD'S PIE

The remains of a roast goose make a really splendid pie. (As my great-aunt observed: 'A fit dinner for a king with a little melted butter.') I make it in the same way as I make the chicken pie described above, except that instead of mushrooms and pimento I put in celery or celeriac, and also raw cooking-apple chopped small—one apple or two, according to the size of the pie. The pie dish should be a shallow one—wide rather than deep—and the potato *purée* covering should be light and frothy with the addition of a spoonful of cream and the beaten white of an egg whisked into it. I smooth this potato top with the back of a spoon (instead of roughing it up with a fork) and then brush it over with melted butter and sprinkle chopped parsley on it. Twenty-five minutes is ample time for it to heat, or the goose will be tough and indigestible.

PIGEONS IN A CASSEROLE

I get large pigeons, because half a big one is enough for one person, and mature birds cooked like this will be tender. I first melt a large chopped onion in oil or bacon fat in a strong saucepan, and when the onion is beginning to colour, I put in the birds and brown them all over. Meanwhile I make the oven hot. The sizzling pigeons are removed, and a sliced apple and banana are put into the hot fat with the onion and coloured, then I stir in a spoonful of flour until it has absorbed the fat, then half a pint of red wine and stir until it is all quite smooth, putting in salt and

Birds

pepper and tasting as it cooks until the seasoning is right—it should be strong. The halved pigeons are put into a casserole which comfortably contains them, the sauce from the pot is poured over them, and the hot *cuisson* of any vegetable is added until the liquid just covers the birds. I then put in a *bouquet garni* and a slice of orange peel, let the dish reach simmering point in the oven, and regulate the heat so that it simmers extremely gently for an hour and forty minutes. The pigeons should be tender when prodded with the point of a sharp knife, and if they are not, let them simmer until they are. I then drain off the liquid into a small saucepan and set it over moderate heat so that it will reduce and thicken, stirring from time to time. The *bouquet* and piece of orange peel are removed, and the thick sauce poured over the pigeons in the casserole, and half a dozen stoned olives are added. This dish can be reheated in its casserole, covered with grease-proof paper firmly attached, for half an hour in a very low oven (280 deg., Gas, No. 1). When I dish up the pigeons, I put a slice of brown bread, one for each, in a hot serving-dish, put a half-pigeon on it, and pour the sauce over them.

This recipe is for two pigeons, and of course the quantity of onions, bananas, apple, and wine must be increased if more are to be cooked. If the pigeons are young ones, I don't divide them. I cook one for each person, and start prodding them for tenderness after one hour in the oven.

ROAST TURKEY

There are two distinct ways of roasting a turkey, and the choice must depend upon the size of the bird and the size of the oven. Given a bird that is easily contained in the oven, by far the simplest and most satisfactory method is to cook it wrapped in aluminium foil, inside which it bastes itself and needs no attention. However, many a vast turkey must somehow be cooked in a rather small oven, and that problem has to be solved in a different way. The stuffing is of course the same in either case.

I stuff my turkey with sausage-meat for the top half, and with chestnut *purée* for the lower half, and experience has taught me

Birds

that a surprisingly large amount of both will be needed, for the inside of a turkey seems like Blackwall Tunnel when you peer into it. To make the chestnut stuffing, I first roast the chestnuts under the grill until the shells split and are easy to remove—or, if I have to prepare a lot of them and turning them under the grill would take too long, I slit each one top and bottom and parboil them for fifteen minutes. Then they must be shelled, and the skin removed too, and the peeled chestnuts are simmered in boiling salted water with a chopped onion for three-quarters of an hour, drained, and minced while still hot. They are mashed with more salt, some pepper, nutmeg, and a good bit of butter well mixed into the warm *purée*, which is put into the vent end of the bird and the gap secured with a cocktail cherry stick. Sausage-meat is put into the neck end, and pushed well down until the cavity is completely filled, but not tightly (or the stuffing would be tough). The point of beginning with the chestnuts is that it is easier to add more sausage-meat than to make more chestnut *purée*, a very tiresome business. The neck opening is fastened with another stick. Large slices of thick fat pork (with the rind cut off) are laid over the entire breast of the bird and firmly attached with string, and two or three snips with scissors are made in the end of each slice to prevent them curling up while cooking.

I spread out a sheet of aluminium foil amply big enough to enclose the turkey, put the bird in the middle of it, and wrap the foil closely, but not tightly, round it, folding over the edges so that there are no gaps and fastening it with pins or string. The parcel is put straight on to the oven shelf, as no roasting-tin is needed, and the oven is set at a moderate heat (350 deg., Gas, No. 4). Taking the total weight of the turkey and its stuffing, I roast it at fifteen minutes to the pound and fifteen minutes extra, and calculate the roasting time so that it is completed about an hour before it is to be dished up. The bird bastes itself splendidly inside its parcel and is left with complete confidence until a quarter of an hour before the end of the time. Then I put a warmed roasting-tin on the kitchen table, take out the parcel, and turn up the heat to hot (420 deg., Gas, No. 7). Gingerly removing the very hot pins from the very hot parcel, I slide the bird and all its

Birds

hot fat into the tin, snip the string and remove it and the bits of pork, and put the tin into the oven for another fifteen minutes, with prepared potatoes in the fat. At the end of this time the bird should be nicely browned. I then take it out and reduce the oven heat to the minimum, turn on the grill, and put the bird into two large sheets of greaseproof paper on the kitchen table. The tin, full of fat and potatoes, goes under the grill to finish cooking them, while I make another parcel of the turkey in the paper, pin it up carefully, and put it back in the oven to keep hot. When the potatoes are done I put them in a buttered dish with a little of their fat, and keep the dish hot over a pan of hot water. I scrape the brown edges of the fat into the tin, add salt and pepper, boil it up for a minute in the tin over heat, and pour into a small double saucepan and leave it to keep hot over hot water. At the final dishing up I strain this gravy through a piece of muslin into a hot sauceboat, which ensures that some of the grease is caught in the muslin. It is a far better gravy than it would be if thickened.

Sometimes I have been faced with the problem of the huge turkey and the small oven. If the oven is deep but not high, the turkey may be too tall to fit into it—this happens with the smaller solid-fuel kitchen stoves. In this case I break the breast-bone of the bird with a well-directed blow from a blunt instrument—a heavy one, a croquet-mallet or the back of a wood chopper. Then the bird can be larded with fat pork and cooked in aluminium foil in the way I have just described. But the carver must look out for little splinters of breast-bone and avoid giving them to people.

On the other hand, a tall oven that is shallow in depth, as they often are in gas stoves and electric ones, may be too small for a big turkey sitting on the shelf, and the door will not shut on it. Then the turkey must be suspended, neck downwards. I tie the legs together very tightly with cord or wire, and take out all the oven shelves except the very top one. Two tiny picture hooks (the kind sold with pins for very light pictures) are hooked over the bars of the top shelf, and the bird suspended from them by the cord or wire round its legs. A dish is put underneath to catch the hot fat which drips out. (By roasting the turkey upside down like this, the breast, which is the driest part of it, will be basted intern-

Birds

ally by fat oozing downwards through the stuffing, and it will be more succulent and better flavoured than it would be if done in the orthodox position.) I set the oven at hot (420 deg., Gas, No. 7) for ten minutes before the bird does into it, and put some bacon fat in the oven dish, and a little water, and a stick or two of celery. I hook the little picture hooks through the leg-tie, and then slip them over the middle rail of the top shelf. The bird is roasted at this strong heat for twenty minutes, during which time I baste it rather often with a long spoon. Then the heat is lowered to a moderate one (320 deg., Gas, No. 3) and the roasting goes on for as many quarters of an hour as there are pounds of turkey (including the weight of the stuffing). As with the other method, I start it in time to have it finished an hour before it is to be eaten. It will have to be basted fairly often while it is cooking. I put the prepared potatoes to roast in the tin three-quarters of an hour before the end of the roasting, and turn them each time that I baste the bird.

Now comes the only difficulty—the removing of the suspended bird, sizzling and slippery with hot fat, from its hooks. I put two large sheets of greaseproof paper on the floor in front of the oven, with long pieces of string underneath them. I pin yesterday's *Times* across my chest with a pin on each shoulder, high enough for it to come up to my chin. I put on rubber gloves, and do my best to feel light-hearted and resolute. Mustering my courage, I open the oven door and take out the dish of potatoes and put it aside. Then, kneeling, as handily as I can I slide the turkey off its hooks and try to clutch the sizzling creature firmly and lower it on to the greaseproof paper. The chances are that it will slip out of my grasp and bounce off the reliable Thunderer which I am wearing as a breast-plate, and I am ready to avert my face in order to avoid annoying burns on the chin. Once the huge, sizzling, slippery bird is safely on the paper, I turn down the oven heat to the minimum, wrap the paper round the bird to make a completely enveloping loose parcel, tie it up, and put it back in the bottom of the oven. I then feel far more light-hearted, deal with the potatoes and the gravy as described above, and go away and forget the whole thing for an hour.

Birds

I never have a second hot vegetable with turkey, only a bowl of plain undressed watercress, and some cold cranberry sauce in a sauce-boat. (Hot cranberry sauce I consider an abomination, and the traditional brussels sprouts seem, to my taste, a little too Teutonic as a flavour combined with those of sausages, chestnuts, and roast bird.)

When the presence of children in the house makes it necessary to roast the turkey for luncheon, I start it a good half-hour earlier than the time indicated by the ordinary calculations; and then, just before leaving for church, I baste it very thoroughly and lower the heat to nearly the minimum (250 deg., Gas, No. $\frac{1}{2}$) and as soon as I return I baste it well again and raise the heat to a little more than the former level for the rest of the cooking (350 deg., Gas, No. 4). The result is much the same, with careful basting—and it is only the unresourceful or the irreligious who protest that cooking and church-going cannot be combined.

If, when all the turkey has been consumed—cold, hashed, and finished in a *mousse*—there is still some remainder stuffing, it can be put into scooped-out tomatoes to make a good dish.

CASSEROLE OF GUINEA FOWL

This bird, tasteless and somewhat flannel-like in texture, can be made pleasing with a little care. I joint it, and brown the pieces in hot bacon fat with finely chopped onion, carrot, and turnip, in a strong pan over moderate heat. Then I put in a spoonful of flour and stir for a minute or two, until the fat is taken up and nothing sticks to the bottom of the pan. Then I add enough hot vegetable stock to cover the pieces, a *bouquet garni*, a piece of orange peel, a pinch of grated root ginger, and salt and black pepper. It is all then turned into a warm casserole, the lid put on, and put into a moderate oven (340 deg., Gas, No. 3) for about two hours, or a little less—it must not be done so long that the pieces of bird fall apart, but very nearly. I dish it up within a border of mashed potato, and have Jerusalem artichokes with it.

Meat Dishes

Beef

BURGUNDIAN STEAK

Thick rump steak, without fat, is necessary for this dish. If I want enough for six people, I buy two pieces of rump steak which will each divide adequately into three, and get the butcher to trim off the outlying bits of fat for me. I buy it the day before I intend to cook it, and marinade it overnight.

Two spoonfuls of bacon fat are put into a strong pan over moderate heat, and when the fat is melted and hot, two small white onions or shallots, two young carrots, a stick of celery, half a small turnip, a clove of garlic and a piece of parsley-root, all chopped small, are put in and melted and stirred until they are soft but not coloured. Meanwhile I drain the steak and divide it into six equal-sized pieces with a sharp knife, and roll them in seasoned flour. They are put into the pot to be gently browned with the vegetables, and I turn them over with care, to avoid making them ragged-looking and to preserve their neat outlines. Red wine (ideally, Burgundy) is then poured in, enough to cover the contents of the pot, and is stirred in very carefully with a wooden spoon, and the bottom of the pot gently scraped for a minute, to ensure that nothing sticks. Then a *bouquet garni* is added, and salt and black pepper, and it is all turned carefully into a warm casserole, the lid put on, and it is put into a fairly hot oven and watched until it just begins to bubble. Then the heat is at once reduced to just enough

Meat Dishes

to keep the liquid at bubbling point, and it is left for two hours. Then I lift out the pieces of steak with a draining spoon and put them on a plate while I pour the liquid through a wire sieve into a small bowl and rub the vegetables through the sieve into it (having removed the *bouquet*). When the sauce is cold I remove the fat from the surface. To reheat this dish, I put, in a shallow buttered ovenproof dish, a piece of stale toasted brown bread under each piece of steak. Three stoned, chopped green olives are put on top of each piece of steak, the sauce is poured over it all, and the dish is covered with two layers of greaseproof paper well fastened down. It is heated in a low oven (300 deg, Gas, No. 2) for half an hour.

STEAK WITH MUSHROOMS

I buy fillet steak for this dish, and marinade it overnight, then drain it, cut it into pieces of a convenient size, and cut off the fat. Four ounces of fat bacon are put into a strong pot over moderate heat until the fat runs freely, and then I add two chopped onions and a crushed clove of garlic and the chopped stalks of half a pound of mushrooms, and stir until the onions are golden. Then I lift out the vegetables and bacon with a draining spoon, pressing them against the sides of the pot so that the fat runs back. The pieces of steak, first rolled in seasoned flour, are then browned gently in the fat and removed. I stir about a spoonful of flour into the fat—as much as is required to make a *roux*—and stir until it is bubbling and browning, and then put in the strained marinade and a glass of red wine, and go on stirring until it is all perfectly smooth. The steak and vegetables and bacon are returned to the liquid, half a pound of mushrooms, broken up, are added, and a *bouquet garni* and salt and pepper. When it reaches simmering point it is put into a casserole with a well-fitting lid and kept at the gentlest simmering point in the oven for two hours. I then take it out, remove the *bouquet*, let the dish get cold and take off the top fat with a spoon. It is reheated in a low oven (300 deg., Gas, No. 2) for half an hour, and a handful of fresh-chopped parsley is stirred into it before serving.

Meat Dishes

STEWED STEAK WITH VEGETABLES

This is a simple, ample stew, for hungry people, and it has to be cooked in a very big casserole. I buy a piece of chuck steak of two pounds or a little more, and as thick as I can get it, I snip off any bits of fat which I can remove without cutting into the main mass, which I leave whole, and marinade overnight. The next day I peel six white onions, six small turnips, six small carrots, and cut into large pieces half a parsnip and three sticks of celery, and crush two cloves of garlic. I make two spoonfuls of oil hot in a strong pan, and carefully brown all these vegetables, and then lift them out with a draining-spoon and put them in a big casserole. The piece of steak, first rolled in seasoned flour, is then browned too, and put in the middle of the casserole with the vegetables round it. I add a little flour to the oil remaining in the pan and stir until it is blended and bubbling, then put in a spoonful of marmalade, the strained marinade, and two spoonfuls of white vinegar, and go on stirring until it is all perfectly smooth. Enough hot vegetable stock is then added as will be needed to cover the contents of the casserole, and the liquid is seasoned with salt, pepper, nutmeg, and a *bouquet garni*; it is all stirred until it simmers, and then poured over the things in the casserole. The lid is put on, and the dish kept at the gentlest simmering point in the oven for three hours, but about half-way through this cooking time I carefully turn over the meat and the larger vegetables, and add, if necessary, a little more hot stock. When it is done I remove the *bouquet*, but I do not degrease this dish. It is reheated for half an hour in a low oven (300 deg., Gas, No. 2), or sometimes for rather longer at a slightly lower heat. The meat is carved into slices in the dish when serving it.

STUFFED FILLET OF STEAK BRAISED

I buy a piece of fillet steak of at least two pounds for this dish, cut off any surplus fat, beat it a bit, and marinade it overnight. The next day I first prepare the stuffing, by chopping *very* small

Meat Dishes

a slice of fat pork, a little white onion, a clove of garlic, half a pimento, and a handful of parsley, and I soak in milk a crustless slice of white bread, and then squeeze out the milk. All this is then pounded together with salt, pepper, nutmeg, a few drops of lemon juice, and a pinch of powdered sage, until it is thoroughly mixed and consolidated. It is then spread on the drained fillet of steak, which is rolled up and tied with string to keep it in a tidy roll. I put two spoonfuls of bacon fat into a strong deep saucepan, and carefully brown the rolled fillet in it when it is hot, and then take it out. Enough chopped onions, carrots, turnips, and celery are then put in to make a layer two inches deep, and stirred and cooked gently until they are quite soft. Then two or three tomatoes, skinned and cut up, are added, and a glass of sherry, and enough hot vegetable stock to cover the vegetables. Seasoning and a pinch of caraway seeds are added and stirred in, and I then put the rolled fillet on top of the gently simmering vegetables, and arrange rashers of fat bacon on it so that its exposed surface is quite covered by them. A round of greaseproof paper is put over the top before the lid goes on, and the pot kept over heat just sufficient to keep the contents simmering, no more, for two and a half hours. Half-way through the cooking time I lift off the slices of bacon, turn over the fillet, and replace the slices, and when doing this I slide a spoon under the layer of vegetables and scrape the bottom of the pot to make sure that nothing is sticking. When done, the fillet is drained and put in a small deep ovenproof dish, without the bacon. The remaining contents of the pot are pressed through a wire sieve and returned to the pot, and enough vegetable stock is added to make this sauce up to about three-quarters of a pint, and salt and pepper and a squeeze of lemon juice are added, according to what it tastes like. A small brown *roux* is made in another pan, and when it is cooked the well-stirred sauce is added gradually (off the fire) and stirred carefully, and then cooked until it is of the consistency of thin cream. It is poured over the fillet, and covered at once with wet greaseproof paper well secured. I reheat this dish with its lid over the paper, for half an hour in a low oven (300 deg., Gas, No. 2), and remember to cut and remove the strings round the fillet before it leaves the kitchen.

Meat Dishes

BRAISED OXTAIL

For six people, I buy two oxtails, because the end-pieces are too small to be dished up, although they are cooked with the rest so that they may contribute their fat and flavour to the whole. I ask the butcher to joint the tails. I chop two white onions, one carrot and one stick of celery, and put them in a pie dish with a crushed clove of garlic, a *bouquet garni* and half a pint of white wine, and marinade the oxtails in this overnight, covered, in order to keep the flavours confined. The next day I make two spoonfuls of oil hot in a large, strong pot, while I drain the contents of the marinade dish. The vegetables are first browned in the hot oil, and then the pieces of oxtail, which are stirred about until they are well browned on all sides. This is done over very moderate heat, because if they were at all scorched they would give the dish a bitter taste. Then everything is removed with a draining-spoon, and the crushed clove of garlic is put into the hot remaining oil, and enough flour is stirred into it to make a thick bubbling *roux*. Then I return the oxtail pieces and vegetables, strain the marinade over them, stir, and add enough hot vegetable stock to cover them, the *bouquet garni*, and four skinned, chopped tomatoes. I stir until all is smooth and free from lumps, season the dish with salt and pepper and a small pinch of mixed spice, and then let it simmer very gently for three hours. Then the *bouquet* is removed, the oxtails and vegetables are lifted out with a draining-spoon into a buttered ovenproof dish, and the liquid strained into a bowl to cool. When it is cold, the top fat is removed. Meanwhile, I have boiled some very young carrots, new potatoes, and little shallots together, lifting them out with a draining-spoon as they are done and, finally, I arrange them round the oxtails in the serving dish, and sprinkle them all with chopped parsley. The degreased sauce from the oxtail is heated gently and more seasoning is added if it needs it; and if it is not thick enough, I mix a teaspoonful of cornflour to the consistency of cream with some sherry, and stir this into the sauce and cook it in a double saucepan until it is smooth and thick. The sauce is then strained over the

Meat Dishes

oxtail and vegetables, and the dish is at once covered with wet greaseproof paper firmly attached. It is reheated, with the lid on over the paper for about forty minutes in a very low oven (280 deg., Gas, No. 1). If it was reheated faster, at a greater heat, the potatoes would disintegrate.

TRIPES COMME CHEZ MOI

Nowadays in England most people recoil from the notion of tripe, probably because they have had it badly prepared and it was slippery on the tongue. This slippery, disagreeable texture can be avoided by washing the stuff in a colander under the cold tap for at least ten minutes, and if this is done thoroughly and the tripe turned over during the process, and then well drained, there should be nothing to grumble at. It is true that tripe has no flavour of its own, but it is a cheap, and superbly digestible, nourishing vehicle for interesting combinations of vegetables. It is good for children, who like it very much.

I blanch a pound of well-washed tripe in boiling salted water for half an hour, then drain it and chop it. Meanwhile I blanch a pound of scrubbed Jerusalem artichokes in the same liquid, and chop them too, when drained. I put two spoonfuls of oil in a wide, strong pot, and when it is hot I cook a large chopped onion in it until it starts to colour. I take it out with a draining-spoon, and put in the artichokes and a chopped and seeded green pepper. These are stirred until the oil is all taken up, and then the tripe and onion are put back, and enough veal broth is added to cover it all. Salt, pepper, and a little lemon juice are added, and when the liquid reaches simmering point, two skinned and chopped tomatoes, and a *bouquet garni*, and the pot left gently simmering for about three hours. Then the *bouquet* is removed and the dish —now fairly consolidated—served with a border of mashed potatoes; or it can be reheated in a low oven (300 deg., Gas, No. 2) for half an hour, and the mashed potato served separately. If digestibility is no object, the mixture can be put into a buttered pie dish and covered with fresh bread-crumbs and bits of butter, and finished under the grill until the crumbs are brown. Tripe can

Meat Dishes

be cooked in this way with other combinations of vegetables, such as parsnips and celery, or the chopped pods of young broad beans with carrots and the addition of some rashers of fat bacon to the initial hot cooking.

CASSEROLE OF LIVER

Half a pound of calf's liver is cut into pieces and rolled in seasoned flour, while a spoonful of bacon fat heats in a strong pan. The liver is lightly browned in the fat, and removed with a draining-spoon, and the remains of the flour—a little more if necessary to take up the hot fat—is also lightly browned in the pan. I then put in half a pint of hot vegetable stock and stir it into the brown *roux* while it heats gently, until it is quite smooth and there are no lumps, and season it with salt and pepper and a pinch of nutmeg. The liver is put into a buttered casserole with two chopped white onions and a peeled, chopped apple and potato, and the sauce poured over it. The casserole is put into a moderate oven and watched until it reaches a gentle simmering point, then the heat is regulated to maintain just that heat for an hour. This dish, which is enough for four people, is best when served straight away and not reheated.

Pork

BRAISED PORK

For six people, I buy two pounds of thick, lean pork, and cut it into six equal-sized pieces to make this excellent Chinese dish. I cut off the fat ends of these pieces, and the edges of the fat at the sides, and melt them in a strong saucepan, very gently, so that gradually they render their fat and become little crisp chunks of crackling. Then I remove them and put them in a casserole which is warming in the oven. Two white onions, a stick of celery and a clove of garlic, all chopped, are cooked in the hot pork fat until they are melted but not coloured, and then taken out with a draining-spoon and put into the casserole, with four peeled,

Meat Dishes

chopped tomatoes. The pieces of pork now have to be *sauté* in the saucepan, and if there is not enough pork fat left to do this, I add a bit of butter and let it get hot before I put in the first pieces of pork. I do them two at a time, turning them so that they are lightly browned on both sides, and transferring them to the casserole when they are done. More butter is put in, as required, between the cooking of each couple of pieces, and made hot before the next two go in. Finally a pinch of grated root ginger is put into the remnant hot fat in the pan, with a spoonful of sherry, and this is cooked to a thin paste, which I spread thinly over each piece of pork in the casserole. These pieces of pork are left without any liquid in the casserole, covered, in a fairly hot oven until the vegetable foundation begins to bubble with the juice of the tomatoes and the incorporated pork fat. Then I season it all with a good sprinkling of salt, pepper, and nutmeg, add two or three bay leaves on top, and cover the casserole with greaseproof paper before putting on the lid. The oven heat is reduced to a very low one (280 deg., Gas, No. 1) and it is left to cook slowly for two hours and a quarter. Then I take out the pieces of pork and put them in a fireproof serving-dish, and discard the bay leaves. I press all the vegetables through a wire sieve, and pour the resulting thin *purée* over the pieces of pork. The dish is carefully covered, and reheated for half an hour in a very low oven (280 deg., Gas, No. 1) for half an hour. Thin slices of lemon are served with it.

COLD PICKLED PORK WITH PRUNES

I ask the butcher to pickle a piece of pork in brine, and the day before I want to use it I wash it well in cold water, then put it in an ample pan with cold water to cover it, and a *bouquet garni*, bring it very slowly to the boil, and simmer it gently, allowing twenty minutes to the pound weight. Then it is drained and left to get perfectly cold. At the same time I have been soaking half a pound of prunes in cold water. The soaked prunes, drained, are simmered in a little cold tea with some sugar and a piece of lemon peel until they are soft but not broken, then they are drained, cooled, and the stones removed with a small pointed knife, as far as

Meat Dishes

possible without wrecking the prunes. When they are cold, a small stoned olive is pushed into the hole of each prune where the stone was. The cold pork is carefully sliced, the rinds cut off the slices, and each slice is cut in half, across it. I then take some cream cheese which has been chilled in the refrigerator—home-made curds do very well, especially if some caraway seeds have been mixed into them—and envelop each stuffed prune with an outer layer of cold, stiff cheese moulded round it, and then wrap a slice of pork round that, and secure it with a cocktail cherry stick. Each of these little objects is then stood on a small slice of buttered rye bread or pumpernickel, and topped with a little bit of red pimento—fresh or tinned. They are arranged on a big dish surrounded with corn salad or curly endive, and chopped chives and parsley are sprinkled generously over everything, and the dish is left in a cold place until it is wanted. I prepare at least two of the objects for each person, with a few to spare, if it is to be the main dish for a cold supper. However, it does excellently well as a savoury, and in that case one is enough for each person.

COLD PICKLED PORK SLICES

I prepare the pickled pork as in the preceding recipe, slice it and cut off the rinds. I make a sauce *verte* (see p. 29) and stiffen it by soaking a spoonful of powdered gelatine in two spoonfuls of cold water, then stirring this together in a double saucepan over heat until it is perfectly dissolved, and, when cool, whisking it into half a pint of sauce *verte* until they are quite amalgamated. This sauce is put into the refrigerator to set. I cook half a pound of chestnuts (as for turkey stuffing, see p. 85) and mix the *purée* thoroughly with four ounces of stoned black olives. I get a large sliced loaf of wholemeal bread, and some fresh Gruyère cheese. I divide slices of the bread lengthwise, making long strips of bread much the same size as the slices of pork. Each strip of bread is rubbed with a crushed clove of garlic, then thinly buttered, and covered with a very thinly cut slice of Gruyère. A layer of the *purée* of olives and chestnuts is spread on the cheese, and a slice of pickled pork put on top of this, then another slice of cheese,

Meat Dishes

another layer of *purée*, and another slice of pork. This is covered with potted shrimps, and the whole thing is then masked with the stiff sauce *verte*. One each of these objects is prepared for each person, and they are served very cold, with a green salad.

Veal

For dishes of veal cooked in a casserole I usually buy the knuckle, and some scrag veal as well if I need more meat than the knuckle will provide (a large one provides enough for four). Fillet of veal is very much more expensive, and the cheaper parts are just as good if they are cooked slowly and carefully. The knuckle-bone makes splendid broth, too. I buy it from the butcher when he is not busy, and when he has chopped the bone into three or four pieces, I ask him to cut the meat off the bones for me, which he does far more neatly and expeditiously than I can. Before cooking the lean meat, I make broth with the bones and the fat scraps, because the broth is usually needed for the preparation of the dish. If I want a brown broth, I brown the bones under the grill for a few minutes before adding them to the fat scraps which have been put to sizzle with a chopped onion in a strong pot; when the fat has shrivelled and the onion is coloured, I put in the bones and a *bouquet garni*, a few slices of carrot, turnip, and celery or parsnip, a slice of lemon peel, and some parsley, and cover all with cold water and add pepper and salt. When the water boils, it is skimmed and the broth then simmered for two hours, strained, and degreased when it is cold.

CASSEROLE OF VEAL WITH SHERRY

A large onion and a clove of garlic, finely chopped, are melted in a strong pot in bacon fat until they are soft and transparent but scarcely coloured. Then the lean meat from a knuckle and a pound of scrag veal is put in and turned in the fat until the pieces are sealed, and then a spoonful of flour is stirred in carefully and cooked until it has absorbed the fat. Next, I pour in, gradually, a teacupful of sherry, and then enough veal broth to cover the meat,

Meat Dishes

stirring gently until there are no lumps and the bottom of the pot is free from floury deposit. Some salt and pepper are added (according to the seasoning of the broth) and three or four skinned, chopped tomatoes, and a *bouquet garni*, and then it is all turned into an ovenproof casserole with a well-fitting lid, and put into a moderate oven until it is simmering. The heat is then reduced so that it just continues to simmer gently for two hours—or perhaps a little longer. I test the veal with the prong of a sharp fork. The *bouquet* is removed when the dish is done, and the lid replaced by wet greaseproof paper while it cools. It can be reheated, with the lid on over the paper, for half an hour in a low oven (300 deg., Gas, No. 2). This is enough for six people.

VEAL AND HAM SOUBISE

I make this dish when I have the remains of a ham, and cut off all the remaining lean meat in small thick pieces. If I haven't got a ham, I ask at a cooked-meat shop for a pound of these pieces, which they are always willing to provide because they are glad to sell the uncarvable remains of one of their cooked hams. Little chunks, rather than slices, are best, and there must not be much fat. For a pound of ham, I use the meat from a large knuckle of veal, and this will be enough for eight people. I butter a big, deep fireproof dish with a lid, and when the pieces of ham and veal, mixed up, have been put in, it ought to be about two-thirds full. I embed a *bouquet garni* (which includes a slice of lemon peel) in the middle of the meat, and then I fill the casserole with *soubise* sauce (see p. 28). I have seasoned the sauce highly with salt and pepper, and I have made plenty of it, because it has to fill the dish almost to the top. The lid is put on, and the dish put into a moderate oven until the sauce is just bubbling, when the heat is reduced to maintain the bubbling stage for two hours, or perhaps a little longer—until the veal is tender when prodded with a sharp fork. Then the bouquet is removed, and the dish covered with wet greaseproof paper. It is reheated with the lid on over the paper, in a very low oven (280 deg., Gas, No. 1) for forty minutes.

Meat Dishes

VEAL WITH MUSHROOMS

I make this dish with a *court bouillon* in which fish has been cooked, and which I have reduced to a *fumet* with the fish bones and trimmings. There must be plenty of it to provide enough *fumet*, and I sometimes buy a cod's head to increase the fish contents of a large *court bouillon*. I get enough pieces of veal, either cut from the knuckle, or scrag, or both, to make an ample dish for as many people as I need it for, and half a pound of mushrooms. I put a spoonful of oil into a strong saucepan, and when it is hot I put in a crushed clove of garlic, and the pieces of veal, which I turn carefully until they are sealed. The veal is then removed with a draining-spoon and the mushrooms, broken up, are put into the remaining hot oil with a spoonful of veal broth, the lid put on, and the pot left over low heat and frequently shaken until the mushrooms are half-cooked. Then they are put with the veal in a buttered casserole, and the fish *fumet* is poured in—enough to cover the contents. No further salt and pepper should be necessary, as the *fumet* will supply ample seasoning. The casserole is put into a moderate oven until the liquid just reaches bubbling point, and the heat is then regulated to keep it at that point for two hours, or until the meat feels tender when tested with a sharp fork. I let it get cold, and then carefully remove the layer of fat on the top with a small spoon. The dish should have become a jelly full of veal and mushrooms. Sometimes I turn it out, if the jelly is stiff enough after being chilled in the refrigerator, and garnish it with watercress and slices of hard-boiled egg; or, if the jelly is not stiff enough to stand, I serve it in the dish, with a salad. But it is just as good hot, when reheated with the lid on the casserole in a low oven (300 deg., Gas, No. 2) for half an hour. If I decide to have this dish and have no fish *fumet*, I buy some cheap, fishy fish, such as a sea bream, and make the *court bouillon*, cook the bream in it, flake off the bream flesh and make the *fumet* with all the rest of it. The bream flakes do for fish-cakes for breakfast, or are accommodated in a thick sauce for luncheon.

Meat Dishes

KNUCKLE BONES (OSSI BUCCHI)

When I buy the large knuckle of veal required for this dish, I ask the butcher to chop it into pieces of about an inch thick, and the meat—fat and lean—is left on the pieces. I roll them in seasoned flour so that they are well coated, and make hot two spoonfuls of oil in a strong pan. The pieces of veal are then cooked in the pan until they are slightly browned all over, along with an onion and a clove of garlic finely chopped. I then put in a glass of white wine, six tomatoes which have been skinned, seeded and chopped, a *bouquet garni,* and enough veal broth or vegetable stock to cover it all. Salt and pepper are added, when the liquid is getting hot, in the quantity which is needed to supplement the seasoning of the broth or stock. The Ossi are then simmered very gently in the pan for an hour and a half, or until the meat is tender when prodded with a sharp fork. Then the *bouquet* is removed, and the fat on the surface taken off when the liquid is cold, and it is all then put into a fireproof serving-dish with a lid, and reheated for half an hour in a cool oven (300 deg., Gas, No. 2). I leave on the kitchen table a saucerful of finely chopped parsley and grated lemon peel, which I sprinkle over the surface just before the dish is served.

The proper accompaniment for the Ossi is not potatoes, but Risotto Milanese (see p. 73), and I reheat it all together in a large dish, with the risotto as a border round the Ossi. The parsley and lemon must be scattered over the middle, not over the border. One knuckle will be enough for four people.

VEAL WITH SAUSAGES AND CHESTNUTS

This good dish from Catalonia involves rather a lot of cooking, but I think it is well worth it. I get two knuckles of veal when I make it for eight people, cut the lean meat off them, and then make a brown veal broth with the bones and fat (see p. 36). When the broth is made—a strong brown broth—I put two spoonfuls of oil in a strong pot, and when it is hot I lightly brown in it the

Meat Dishes

pieces of veal. Then I sprinkle in a spoonful or more of flour, and stir until the flour has quite absorbed the oil and is beginning to colour. This stirring must be gently done, in order to avoid making the meat ragged. I have ready a finely chopped onion, clove of garlic, and leek (only the white part) and these I now put in, with a glass of white wine, half a pound of skinned, chopped tomatoes, three bay leaves, and enough of the veal broth to cover it all. I stir it gently but thoroughly, and when it comes to the boil I leave it to simmer slowly for an hour and a half, or a little longer if the meat is not absolutely tender. Meanwhile I have put half a pound of the smallest chippolata sausages in a pan over moderate heat, and cook them carefully until they are browned all over but not overdone. They are taken out and drained when they are done. While all this is going on I cook a pound of chestnuts, first slitting them at both ends, blanching them in boiling water for ten minutes, and then removing their shells and inner skins. They are simmered for nearly an hour in vegetable stock with a chopped onion, and then drained when they are tender but not soft. (The *cuisson* makes an excellent foundation for soup.) When the veal is done, the bay leaves are removed, and the cooked, drained sausages and chestnuts are added, and stirred carefully into the sauce until all is well mingled. It is then turned into a buttered casserole, and reheated, with wet greaseproof paper covering the dish under its lid, in a low oven (280 deg., Gas, No. 1 or a bare 1½) for forty minutes. It must be served very hot, and is delicious.

GOULASCH OF VEAL

This, emphatically, is not a dish for the Britons who object to 'greasy foreign food'. Before starting to cook it I put a small pinch of saffron in a cup to soak in a spoonful of water, and stir it occasionally until it is quite dissolved. Meanwhile I cut up four rashers of fat bacon and let them cook gently with a chopped onion and clove of garlic until most of the fat has come out and the vegetables are soft and transparent but not brown. Then I put into this pan a pound of veal scrag, cut into pieces, and brown the pieces slightly with the vegetables. Four skinned, chopped

Meat Dishes

tomatoes are then added, and a chopped seeded pimento, and the dissolved saffron, and all is cooked very gently together for a few minutes. Then a glass of white wine and a handful of washed sultanas is added, and when it all reaches bubbling point it is turned into a buttered casserole and left simmering in the oven for an hour and a half, being stirred occasionally to ensure that the sultanas are equally distributed and absorbing the fat. This dish is enough for four people and can be reheated with the lid on, in a low oven (300 deg., Gas, No. 2) for half an hour.

BRAISED FILLET OF VEAL

I get the butcher to cut pieces of the size and number I need, from the fillet of veal about half an inch thick, and then to flatten them for me until they are somewhat larger and thinner. (I get one good-sized piece for each person.) I rub each piece on both sides with a cut clove of garlic first, then with a cut lemon, and dip them in seasoned flour. For each piece of veal I take one shallot, one small carrot, a slice of turnip, a half-stick of celery, and two mushrooms, and chop them all up. These chopped vegetables are then melted—but not at all browned—in two spoonfuls of hot oil in a strong pan, and when they are done they are removed with a draining-spoon, pressed against the side of the pan to express the fat, and put into a buttered casserole in a low oven. Then the pieces of veal are carefully turned and sealed, one by one, in the remainder of hot oil. Meanwhile I have poured into the casserole enough white wine to contain the vegetables, but scarcely to cover them. A *bouquet garni* is embedded in the middle, and the pieces of veal are put on top of this bed of vegetables, which has been seasoned with salt and pepper first. The casserole is covered with buttered paper before the lid is put on, and the oven heat is raised slightly until the vegetables are just simmering in the wine. The heat is then regulated to maintain this gentle simmering, for two hours, but once or twice during that time I rearrange the pieces of veal, so that the lower layer ends up on top, and all have been turned over. If, in the course of the cooking, the vegetables seem to lack liquid, I pour in a little more wine.

Meat Dishes

At the end of two hours, I put into the casserole six or eight lettuce leaves which have been washed and dried and broken up, and leave the dish to cook for another half-hour. Then I take out the pieces of veal and put them on a sieve to drain, and press all the vegetables through a coarse wire sieve. This *purée* is then mixed with Béchamel sauce (see p. 25) in the proportion of a spoonful of the sauce for each cupful of *purée*, and the warm sauce is thoroughly stirred into it. The pieces of veal are arranged in a big, shallow fireproof dish and the thickened *purée* is poured over them, and the dish is covered at once with wet greaseproof paper. It is reheated in a low oven (280 deg., Gas, No. 1½) for half an hour or a little longer.

Mutton

Mutton is, I think, the least manageable meat for a cook to dress for a dinner prepared in advance. There is always a lot of fat which must be removed, because although mutton fat is delicious if the meat has been grilled or roasted, it is disagreeably dull and greasy when cooked slowly unless strong and spicy flavours are introduced as in the regional cooking of North Africa, or unless there is starchy vegetable matter to absorb it, as there is in Irish Stew and Lancashire Hotpot. The natural flavour of mutton seems to me to demand garlic in considerable quantities.

LAMB CUTLETS WITH TOMATOES AND MUSHROOMS

The cutlets have to be trimmed so that there is almost no fat left on them, and the upper part of the bone is scraped bare. For six people, I buy twelve cutlets and two pounds of tomatoes and a pound of mushrooms. (This is a dish for the early autumn, when both tomatoes and mushrooms are cheap.) I wash the mushrooms and leave them whole, and I blanch, skin, seed, and chop the tomatoes. I butter a deep casserole, and put a layer of mixed tomato and mushrooms in it, and then six cutlets on top of that, and sprinkle over them plenty of salt and pepper, and a clove of garlic very finely chopped up. Then another layer of tomatoes and

Meat Dishes

mushrooms covers the cutlets, then the rest of the cutlets, more salt and pepper and chopped garlic, a small pat of butter is put on each cutlet, and a handful of finely chopped parsley is scattered over the top. The lid of the casserole should fit well. It is cooked in a low oven (300 deg., Gas, No. 2) for two and a half hours. This dish is such a simple one to prepare that I usually get it ready in the morning, and put it into the oven two and a half hours before dinner. However, it may be reheated, with the lid on, for forty minutes in a lower oven (280 deg., Gas, No. $1\frac{1}{2}$). The remains of this dish jellify, and form an excellent cold thing for luncheon or supper; and so I sometimes cook it in larger quantities in the first place, and if the dinner guests do not scoff the lot when invited to have some more, there is the residue as a ready-made cold dish for the next day. (If put to chill in the refrigerator, it will turn out on to a dish and stand up.)

MOCK VENISON OF COLD MUTTON

This is the late Mrs. C. S. Peel's delicious way of disguising the remains of a cold joint of mutton. (Roast mutton, naturally — I had better declare at once that I consider boiled mutton uneatable.) A marinade is prepared, of a chopped onion and clove of garlic, the juice of a lemon, two spoonfuls of sherry, a spoonful of mushroom ketchup, a spoonful of marmalade, salt and pepper and four cloves. All this is well mixed together in a pie dish until the marmalade has dissolved in the liquid, and then rather thick slices of cold roast mutton, without any fat, are put in to soak for several hours, and turned occasionally. (I put in all the lean scraps that I can cut off the joint, even quite small bits, when I have carved all the tidy slices.) When they are well marinaded, the pieces of mutton are put in a strainer over the pie dish to drain. Then the marinade is strained into a saucepan and warmed, while a small brown *roux* is prepared and cooked. The marinade is stirred into the *roux* to make a brown sauce, with the addition of a little vegetable *cuisson* if the liquid is not quite enough, and when this sauce is cooked and thickish, it is poured over the pieces of mutton in a buttered fireproof dish, and covered at once with wet

Meat Dishes

greaseproof paper. The dish is reheated, with the lid on over the paper, for half an hour in a low oven (280 deg., Gas, No. 1½).

The remains of roast veal, or of roast turkey legs, can be accommodated equally well in this fashion.

COLD STUFFED SHOULDER OF LAMB

I always cook this the day before I want it. When I buy the shoulder of lamb—as large a one as possible—I ask the butcher to bone it for me, and of course I take the bone too, for soup. (If the butcher is obviously too busy to be asked to do the boning, I can do it myself almost as neatly, by sliding a sharp little knife round the bone very carefully.) I make the stuffing by soaking two slices of bread in milk which has been seasoned, squeezing them dry, and mixing them with some onion, garlic, and mushrooms which have all been chopped and melted in hot oil and then drained. This mixture is pounded together with a pinch of nutmeg, a squeeze of lemon juice, and some more salt and pepper. I then stuff it into the cavity in the joint, pressing it in firmly, and secure the meat round it with cocktail cherry sticks. The joint is then *piqué* with one or two cloves of garlic, according to its size, and roasted with some good dripping in a hot oven (410 deg., Gas, No. 6) and basted fairly often until it is done. It is then left to get cold overnight. When dishing it up, I first carve it in slices, and arrange them flat on a large dish, and put a little chopped gherkin, and chopped parsley, and chopped hard-boiled egg, on each slice, and surround the slices with a border of watercress or endive.

RAGOUT OF MUTTON

For this dish I get two breasts of mutton, boned, and cut off all the fat. Then I divide each one into three pieces, and flatten them. Two large onions and a large clove of garlic are chopped, and cooked slowly in hot oil until they are slightly browned, when they are removed with a draining-spoon. Then the pieces of mutton are browned in the oil until they are decidedly sizzling, and then removed. Enough flour is stirred into the remaining oil

Meat Dishes

to absorb it, and then two chopped, skinned tomatoes are added, and all is stirred together for a minute or two. Then it is turned into a buttered casserole with the onion and garlic and pieces of mutton and a *bouquet garni*, salt and pepper, and enough vegetable *cuisson* to cover everything. It is brought slowly to simmering-point in the oven, and the heat is then regulated to keep it simmering quite gently for an hour and a half. Meanwhile I cook a pound of young carrots with seasoning and some chopped parsley, and a pound of peas with seasoning and a chopped shallot, and then drain these vegetables. When the mutton is cooked it is not drained, but any surplus liquid in the casserole is taken out with a spoon, and the vegetables are put in and mixed with the meat, etc. This dish can be reheated, well covered, in a low oven (280 deg., Gas, No. 1½) for twenty minutes, or half an hour.

BOSNIAN STEW

For this dish I buy about two pounds of best end of neck of mutton or lamb, and leave all the fat on the cutlets when I have divided them. I make it with the *cuisson* of any strongly flavoured vegetable—turnip, or celery, or Jerusalem artichoke. First, I put a pinch of saffron to soak in a spoonful of the *cuisson* until it is soft and can be dissolved by stirring, while the rest of the *cuisson* is being warmed. Then I heat a spoonful of oil in a strong pot, and put into it two onions, a clove of garlic, and four skinned tomatoes, all chopped, and the dissolved saffron. This is stirred until it is a soft mass, and then the cutlets are added, and two leeks which have been washed and chopped up. Salt and pepper are sprinkled over all this, and the *cuisson* poured over it until it is covered. It is simmered gently for an hour or so—until the meat is done. It will keep hot for a long time in a warm corner of the stove, but it can be reheated in a buttered casserole with all its liquid, for half an hour in a low oven.

COUSCOUS

This is the famous Arab dish that keeps on cropping up in travellers' tales. Queasy English wanderers have been relating ever

Meat Dishes

since the eighteenth century how they supped with a courteous sheik in some grim stronghold, and how they managed to repress a shudder when their host dipped his fingers in the great dish of greasy mutton and offered to them the sheep's eyeball as the tidbit of honour. I have eaten couscous in Morocco, but was never troubled with eyeballs, because for one thing I was not a guest of honour, and in any case the head of the sheep was not a part of the dish. It is in my opinion the best mutton stew ever concocted —very greasy indeed, but then mutton is naturally greasy food, and Arab cooks contrive to make the grease delicious.

I have adapted the classic Arab method of cooking this dish to suit European tastes, and taken considerable liberties with it. For one thing, the couscous itself—the farinacious foundation or covering of the meat—is usually bought in the *Souk*, already prepared. If it is made at home, semolina is used instead; and this is made into a springy dough with water and then steamed over the pot in which the meat is cooking, and afterwards worked up with butter. It is not boiled or baked, only steamed, and when finished it still tastes to me like raw, moist dough, and I don't like it. So I have substituted for it a semolina paste like gnocchi, made with the same ingredients, but ending up cooked instead of raw. And I have omitted some of the herbs and seasonings which can be bought in a North African *Souk* but are not found in English gardens or greengrocers' shops.

I put about a pound and a half of mutton (neck or breast, cut in large pieces) in a deep, strong saucepan, with a handful of parsley, four onions, four carrots, and one turnip, all chopped. The seasoning consists of a spoonful of chopped chervil, a good pinch of saffron, four teaspoonfuls of salt, two of black pepper, and two of ground root ginger. (This sounds an alarmingly large amount of pepper and ginger, but their 'hot' quality is quite absorbed by the fat in cooking.) Then four ounces of butter and a pint and a half of water are added, the pot is brought slowly to the boil, and simmered for an hour and a half. Then four sliced *courgettes* (baby marrows) and a handful of washed raisins are put in, and the simmering continued for another half-hour. Meanwhile I boil in another pan a pint of water and four ounces of

Meat Dishes

butter with some salt, and when the butter is melted, sprinkle in gradually four ounces of semolina, stirring well to make sure that there are no lumps. When it is smooth and cooked and begins to leave the sides of the pan, I spread it over the bottom of a buttered casserole and let it get cold. When the mutton is cooked, I put it, and all the solid vegetable contents of the cooking pot, on this semolina base, and also about eight spoonfuls of the liquid in the pot, scooping it up from the bottom with a ladle so as to include the rich, spicy residue which tends to sink. It is reheated, well covered, in a low oven (300 deg., Gas, No. 2) for forty minutes. No potato or other vegetable should be served with it.

If *courgettes* are out of season, cucumber may be used instead.

MDERBEL

This is another delicious and very greasy Moorish way of cooking mutton. I put about a pound and a quarter of neck or breast of mutton, cut in large pieces, in a deep strong pot with a large chopped leek, two teaspoonfuls of salt, one of ground root ginger, a pinch of saffron, a pint of olive oil and half a pint of water. It is brought slowly to the boil, and simmered very gently for two hours. Meanwhile, I peel and cut in thin slices a pound of pumpkin, and cook them in another saucepan in four spoonfuls of very hot oil, until they are thoroughly browned but not in the least burned. When they are quite done I drain them well, crush them in a bowl, and mix with them two teaspoonfuls of powdered cinnamon and two of castor sugar. The cooked mutton and leeks are removed from the pot to a buttered casserole with a draining-spoon, and the liquid that remains in the pot is poured into the bowl with the pumpkin mixture, well stirred, and it is all then put on top of the meat. The dish is reheated, well covered, in a low oven (300 deg., Gas, No. 2) for half an hour. It is enough for four people. When I make it for six, I increase the quantity of mutton, and of pumpkin and leek, but I find that the same amount of oil and seasoning is quite adequate.

The rich remains of these spicy, greasy dishes are ideally suitable for making a dish of spaghetti the next day (see p. 66).

Various Hot Supper Dishes

These are dishes which cannot be reheated without spoiling them, but which can be cooked and finished half an hour before they are to be eaten, after which time they will keep hot very well in a cool oven until they are needed. They are convenient things to prepare for luncheon, or for informal evening meals, especially for unexpected guests, as they are made with materials which are often available in cupboard or larder when there is not enough meat or fish to eke out for the sudden arrivals.

CASSEROLE OF SAUSAGES AND ONIONS

I chop a pound of onions and two cloves of garlic and melt them in two spoonfuls of hot oil in a strong saucepan, taking care to cook them gently until they are only faintly coloured, then transfer them to a casserole and put a pound of chippolata sausages, pricked, on top of them. The casserole is put, uncovered, in the top part of a moderate oven (340 deg., Gas, No. $3\frac{1}{2}$) for about an hour and a half, or until the sausages are browned all over. They must be turned over from time to time, and when turning them I scrape the bottom of the casserole to ensure that the onion is not sticking to it. Then I drain off all the fat into a pan, pressing the onions firmly, and the sausages lightly, against the side of the casserole to get all the fat out of them. A spoonful of port and a pinch of grated nutmeg is stirred into the fat, and when it begins to bubble in the pan, enough flour to make it into a *roux*. The

Various Hot Supper Dishes

roux, when cooked, is diluted with enough hot stock of any kind to make it into a sauce of the consistency of thin cream, and salt and pepper are put in according to the seasoning of the stock. When the sauce is cooked it is poured over the contents of the casserole, which can be kept hot over a pot of hot water, or at the bottom of a very low oven. Chippolatas are best for this dish, but ordinary sausages will do at a pinch.

SAUSAGES WITH CHESTNUTS

I once made this dish for unexpected guests when there was nothing in the larder except chippolata sausages, chestnuts, and tomatoes, and it was too late to buy anything else. I put the chestnuts in a well-greased baking tin in a hot oven (440 deg., Gas, No. 8) until they were roasted and splitting, then took them out and shelled and skinned them (wearing rubber gloves and working gingerly and fast). I put them back in the tin with halved tomatoes between them, put a cake rack over the tin, and put a pound of pricked chippolata sausages on it. I salted and peppered the chestnuts and tomatoes, and put the tin and the rack back in the oven and reduced the heat to a moderate one (350 deg., Gas, No. $3\frac{1}{2}$) and kept an eye on the sausages until they were done, turning them occasionally. The fat that dripped out of them cooked the chestnuts and tomatoes to perfection. I put the chestnuts and tomatoes in a hot dish, sprinkled plenty of chopped parsley and chives over them, and put the chippolatas on top, and kept the dish hot with its lid on at the bottom of the oven with the heat at the minimum while I had the drink which I felt I had deserved.

HAM AND EGGS WITH CREAMED KALE

For six people, I cook two pounds of kale as described on p. 124 and put it in a thick layer in a large shallow fireproof dish. I then grill very slightly on both sides six slices of ham, and arrange them on the kale, pressing each one down so that it makes a sort of shallow saucer. Then I put an *œuf mollet* (see p. 42) on each slice

Various Hot Supper Dishes

of ham. If I want to keep the dish hot with a lid on it for a short time in the oven, I put a bit of butter on each egg to prevent the ham becoming too dry.

BARLEY WITH VEGETABLES

This is a dish to make in an emergency when there is no meat, fish, or even eggs or sausages to cook, and it is stodgy but sustaining and delicious. All that is required is pearl barley, pieces of fat bacon, stock or vegetable *cuisson* of any kind, and a few different vegetables of the solid (not leaf) varieties. For six people (I cook plenty of it as it is to be their main supper dish) I cut up five or six ounces of fat bacon scraps and melt them gently in a strong deep pan. When the fat has mostly come out, I put in two large chopped onions and one chopped clove of garlic, and let them melt but not brown. Meanwhile a pot of stock or vegetable *cuisson* is warming. When the onions are beginning to colour, I stir into them half a pound of pearl barley, and stir until the barley has taken up the fat, then add two skinned chopped tomatoes and stir for a minute or two longer. Then hot stock is poured in, stirred until the barley is just simmering in it, plenty of salt, pepper, and grated nutmeg is scattered over it and stirred in, and the pot is left to simmer. It must be stirred from time to time, and more stock added as it absorbs it. The cooking must continue until the barley is really soft and fluffy, and this takes about an hour and a half—unless it is done in a double saucepan, in which case it will take about three hours, but will need almost no stirring, only the occasional addition of extra stock. Before the cooking is finished, I collect such vegetables as are available—celery, carrots, Jerusalem artichokes, broad beans, peas, *courgettes*, green peppers, mushrooms, leeks—whatever happens to be in season, and cook them together very gently in butter and a little stock, with plenty of salt and pepper and a couple of skinned chopped tomatoes. (Of course the solid ones are chopped first.) This mass of mixed vegetables is simmered and stirred until it is quite soft and forms a thick *purée* which has absorbed all the butter and stock. When the barley is perfectly cooked and not at all sloppy, it is turned into a buttered casserole

Various Hot Supper Dishes

and the vegetable *purée* is spread over the surface of it. Then I cover the vegetable layer thickly with grated cheese, and put little bits of butter here and there on the top, and put the casserole in the top of a warm oven (340 deg., Gas, No. 3) until the cheese begins to brown. This takes about a quarter of an hour.

Mousses and *Pâtés*

I prefer to call food by English names when I can, but the English for 'mousse' is 'shape', or 'mould', in the dismal dictionary of English kitchens. It is always difficult to know what to call the stuff that one cooks, because it seems affected to use French terms, but the English ones do sound a little sad. The words hash, mince, mould, shape, sponge, fritter, and batter come echoing back from a stodged past—and they look, and sound, anti-aperitive. Even the few imaginative and 'folksy' names for English food, such as Toad-in-the-Hole and Bubble-and-Squeak, convey a grim suggestion of mediaeval medicaments. ('Take of newts two drachms, and pound with a toad's liver, and stinkwort culled on a moonless night. . . .') I remember being invited by a girl whose spelling was not her strong point, to a meal which she promised would consist of 'just a mouse and a cold sweat'. (But the French, whose skill with food has made their culinary terms of art universal, call some of their dishes by very odd names. The classic French cookery book of Tante Marie, the Mrs. Beaton of France, has a recipe for *beignets soufflés* with the sub-title *pets de nonne*.) It is certainly better to call dishes by proper names, such as Melba or Marengo, which sound triumphant and convey no nauseating hints. I wish I had the courage to call dishes of my own contriving Churchill or Matapan—but I have not.

MOUSSE OF HARE

I get the hare jointed and wash and dry it, and marinade it

Mousses and *Pâtés*

overnight. The drained joints are browned in hot oil with some chopped onion in a deep strong pot, and I then put in a cupful of port, some salt, pepper and a *bouquet garni* and enough hot vegetable *cuisson* to cover the joints. The pot is brought gently to the boil, skimmed, and simmered for two hours, then the hare is removed and left to drain on a sieve, and the *cuisson* is strained; I keep the residue of onion, and discard the *bouquet*. I bone the cold joints and put the meat through the mincer with the onion, and a slice of white bread, two cloves of garlic, two small carrots, and a very small turnip. All this minced material is put into a bowl, it is seasoned with salt and pepper, and the juice of half a lemon, and when it has been well stirred, two beaten eggs are mixed with it thoroughly. I butter a basin which will just contain the mixture, fill it compactly, and cover it with a layer of buttered greaseproof paper, and then with an unbuttered one. The paper is tied down tightly with string, and the *mousse* is steamed for two hours in a saucepan with simmering water within an inch of the top of the basin. I make a thick sauce with a small brown *roux* and half a pint of the strained *cuisson*, and season it with a pinch of nutmeg and as much salt and pepper as seems necessary. If the *mousse* is to be hot, I start to steam it only two and a half hours before dinner, turn it into a serving-dish, when it is done, and keep it hot in the bottom of the oven under a very large inverted flower-pot lined with buttered paper, while the sauce is being kept hot in a double saucepan, to be poured over the *mousse* just before it is served. If I have the *mousse* cold, I make a Cumberland sauce (see p. 29) and put it in a sauce-boat. (But I usually make sauce with the hare *cuisson* in any case, and use it hot to contain *œufs mollets* at another meal, or as the foundation of an excellent dish of scraps and spaghetti.)

TURKEY MOUSSE

When I have carved everything that I can get off the turkey, there is always enough left to make a *mousse* out of the little uncarvable scraps. Having cut off every bit of meat on the top half of the bird, I turn it upside down, and remove the excellent fat

Mousses and *Pâtés*

meat that is found underneath. Finally, I break open the carcass, and remove useful strips of meat from the ribs and from various other crannies between bones. I remove also the remainder of the stuffing of chestnut and sausage-meat, and keep these separate. I mince the bits of turkey, see how much I have got, and make a corresponding quantity of mince with some of both kinds of stuffing, some raw onion and carrot, two raw cloves of garlic and a piece of raw turnip, and some crumb of wholemeal bread. I then mix all this minced stuff together in a large bowl with plenty of salt and black pepper, a pinch of nutmeg, a pinch of mixed spice, the juice of half a lemon, and two beaten eggs. (If there is a lot of the minced material—enough to fill a quart basin—I use three, or even four, beaten eggs.) When it is all thoroughly mixed, I press the mixture gently but firmly into a buttered basin which will just contain it, and cover it with buttered greaseproof paper. Then I put another layer of greaseproof paper over that, tie both on firmly, and steam the *mousse* in a saucepan for an hour, or for forty minutes in a pressure-cooker. Meanwhile, I make a sauce with a quarter of a pound of mushrooms, broken up very small, which I cook gently in butter with a spoonful of stock until they are quite soft and have almost absorbed their *cuisson*. They are then stirred into half a pint of thick Béchamel sauce with their remaining juices, seasoned with salt, pepper, and a squeeze of lemon juice, stirred until all is unified, and kept hot in the double saucepan over hot water. When the *mousse* is done it is turned out on to a dish and kept hot in the oven well covered with grease- proof paper. The sauce is poured over it when dishing up.

If I have the *mousse* cold, I do not make a sauce, but glaze it with an aspic jelly made with half a pint of very clear stock from the turkey carcass and a little sherry, flavoured with lemon juice and garlic, and set with two-thirds of a pint packet of powdered gelatine, or two and a half leaves of leaf gelatine dissolved carefully in very little water. The hot aspic is strained into a bowl, and when it has almost, but not absolutely, set, I spread it gradually over the cold *mousse* with a wet palette-knife and when the remains of the aspic is quite cold I chop it and put it round the *mousse* in

Mousses and *Pâtés*

the dish, with a little chopped parsley and bright scraps of red pepper or tomato for decoration.

MOUSSE OF VEAL

First of all I cook half a pound of mushrooms, broken very small, in butter and a little stock until they are soft, and then drain them. Then I make a pint of *poulette* sauce (see p. 27). Then I mince a pound of lean scrag veal and a slice of white crumb bread, one shallot, one clove of garlic, and a small seeded pimento. (If this is tinned, it has to be well drained first.) All this minced material is mixed together thoroughly in a bowl with salt, pepper, a pinch of nutmeg and the juice of half a lemon, and then enough of the *poulette* sauce is stirred into it to produce a mixture of the consistency of thick porridge. Then the two whites of egg left after making the *poulette* sauce, well whisked, are folded into the mixture, and it is put into a buttered basin which will contain it without its reaching quite to the top. Buttered greaseproof paper is put over it, and then another layer of the paper, they are tied down firmly, and the *mousse* is steamed for two hours in a saucepan, or for one hour in a pressure-cooker. It is turned out into a hot dish when it is done and served as soon as possible, with the *poulette* sauce (which has been warmed in its double saucepan) poured over it.

If, however, I intend to have the *mousse* cold, I leave it in the basin overnight, and turn it out the next day, and mask it with the *poulette* sauce. If this is not stiff enough to spread with a palette-knife, I whip a little cream slightly, put it into the sauce and whip it all together until the sauce is firmer. I spread it over the *mousse* as smoothly as I can with the palette-knife, and smooth it with the back of a spoon, decorate the top with snippets of red pepper or tomato and lemon peel, to make a red and yellow pattern of some sort. The *mousse* is put in the refrigerator until it is wanted, and served surrounded with watercress.

LE PÂTÉ DE LA COMTESSE DE PREUX

This delicious dish dates from the days when game was cheap

Mousses and *Pâtés*

and plentiful, and I used always to make it before Christmas. Nowadays it is an extravagance, but I still make it sometimes because everyone likes it, and it is a wonderful stand-by for Christmas-time entertaining. It is made of one hare, two old partridges, and four pigeons; and half a pound of fat pork with no lean at all. I get the poulterer to joint the hare.

First I cut off every bit of meat from the hare. Then I cut up the partridges, carving the breasts whole and then divide each breast into two, and then cut off all the rest of the flesh from the birds, finally turning them upside down to get at further morsels underneath. Then I deal with the pigeons in exactly the same way. (This cutting-up of raw game is a troublesome business, and I find that the best way is to do it with a small sharp knife and one's fingers. A carving-knife and fork are not the right tools.) I put aside the pieces of the birds' breasts; and all the rest of the meat from the birds, and the hare, and also the fat pork, I put through the mincer, twice. I then mix all this minced material in a large bowl with plenty of seasoning—a teaspoonful of salt and one of black pepper, a good pinch of grated nutmeg and the juice of half a lemon—scattered over it gradually as it is stirred. I have ready a large, shallow fireproof dish (with a very well-fitting lid) and butter the dish carefully. When the minced meat is thoroughly well mixed with its seasoning, a layer of it is put into the dish, and then the pieces of the birds' breasts are arranged on it—half the total number of pieces—then more mince, then the rest of the pieces, and then a final layer of mince. All this material must be pressed down very firmly indeed until it is a firm solid mass. The incorporated pieces must not show on the surface, which should be perfectly flat and firm and smooth, and at least half an inch lower than the rim of the dish. Four thick slices are cut from a very large onion, each slice is stuck with four cloves, and the slices put on the surface of the *pâté*. I then pour in four spoonfuls of brandy, and put on the lid. This is sealed with a little wettish flour-and-water dough, pressed all along the rim of the dish, where the lid joins it. The dish is put into a low oven (320 deg., Gas, No. 2) for four hours. The lid is left sealed for twenty-four hours, then the paste is scraped off, the lid removed, and the slices of onion taken out.

Mousses and *Pâtés*

This *pâté* ought not to be put into the refrigerator. It will keep perfectly for a fortnight in a cool place. It is not meant to be turned out, but should be left in its *terrine* and carved in thin slices with a sharp knife, and eaten with fresh toast and butter, as it is a *pâté terrine*.

Excellent soup can be made with the carcasses of the birds, and of the hare (see p. 38) in considerable quantities—so it is not such a very extravagant dish after all.

PÂTÉ DE VEAU EN CROUTE

This is a *pâté* enclosed in a pastry crust, and is made of a pound of veal scrag and a pound of fresh pork. These have to be marinaded overnight. First I cut off all the fat from the lean of both veal and pork, cut the lean meat into thin slices, and put it into a marinade consisting of a glass of white wine, two spoonfuls of oil, a chopped onion and a crushed clove of garlic, salt, pepper and a pinch of mixed spice, all well mixed together before the slices of meat are put in. I cover the dish, and put it in a cold place. Then I chop all the fat meat small, and put it into a marinade made in the same way, with the addition of an extra clove of garlic and some parsley and chervil. This dish is then covered and put beside the first one. Next, I make the pastry, by sieving one and a half pounds of plain flour and a teaspoonful of salt, into a large bowl, and working into it six ounces of butter and six of lard with a teacupful of cold water and, finally, one beaten egg. When it is a firm, elastic dough, thoroughly worked, I wrap it loosely in paper and put it into the refrigerator. I do all this the day before I mean to cook the *pâté*, and two days before it is needed.

The next day, I remove the bits of onion and other vegetable matter from the two marinades, and drain the meat, still keeping lean and fat separate. I roll out the dough into an oblong about a quarter of an inch thick, and put half the fat meat on it. Then all the lean meat is arranged on this layer, and then the rest of the fat meat on top of that. The meat must not come within an inch of the edge of the dough all round, and this bare edging of dough is brushed with cold water. Then I fold in the dough over the meat

Mousses and *Pâtés*

—sides first, then bottom and top, like an envelope—so that it encloses the meat completely in a fat, but flattish, oblong parcel. I pinch the joins firmly together with finger and thumb, and put it, the other way up, on a greased and floured baking tin. I make a hole in the middle of it, of the size of a sixpence, and put the tin into a fairly hot oven (380 deg., Gas, No. 5) for about an hour and a half. I keep an eye on it in the later stages of the baking, and as soon as I see decided puffs of steam coming out of the hole, I know that it is done. (People who like pastry to look bronzed and glossy should brush it over with beaten egg before baking it. I don't.)

It is eaten cold on the following day, with a green salad, and is enough for six people. (Tante Marie observes that some people prefer their *pâtés* hot, but adds sternly that they should be served cold nevertheless, as they are then *moins indigeste*.)

I never throw away the marinade after making this dish, but use it for cooking soaked lentils or dried peas or beans to make a *purée* for some other meal.

Vegetables

I would almost always rather have any vegetables by themselves as a separate course if I could, except potatoes—and I don't much like potatoes anyway. Most of the dishes of meat or birds in this book are cooked with vegetables of some kind and so are flavoured with them. I don't think that much is achieved by the addition of, say, a leek in white sauce to a helping of veal cooked in sherry, with mushrooms, except a silly confusion of flavours and too much on the plate. Of course the standard English diet of 'plain roast or boiled' does demand the taste and succulence of vegetables to ameliorate the monotony of mutton and beef which tastes only of itself or even of nothing at all by the time that the cook has boiled or roasted the essential flavours out of it. Here lies the reason for the English habit of insisting on 'two veg' with every meat dish, but it seems to me a mistake to persist in this habit when the meat has been cooked with vegetables and appears as a succulent dish. Good bread is a far better accompaniment to meat, in my opinion, than boring boiled potatoes or villainously indigestible fried ones; and a salad on a side plate contrasts but does not conflict with the flavours of meat that is meant to taste of something. However, it does add complications to the cook-hostess dinner-party to have a vegetable as a separate course, and so, very often, it has to accompany the main course. If, however, this is a boneless and unmessy one, so that the plates are fairly clear when it has been eaten, a vegetable that has been kept warm in a hot-water dish on the sideboard can then be produced and eaten after, instead of with, the meat.

Vegetables

POTATOES

New potatoes, boiled with mint, and drained and oiled with butter and sprinkled with chopped parsley, are certainly very nice little vegetables, and go well with most dishes. Roast potatoes are delicious when done under the turkey. A turkey is about the only thing that I ever roast, and so I have nothing to say about other roast potatoes, except that I don't eat them. Mashed potatoes, very carefully prepared, are useful to absorb good sauce or gravy, especially as most people seem to be so very prim about making sops with their bread. But these potatoes must be as different as possible from the grey, lumpy stodge which is recklessly piped into little fancy rosettes and wedded with watery cabbage in the dismal 'two veg' union of our Islands.

MASHED POTATOES

I prepare half a pound of potatoes for each person, and cut them in half—or in four if they are big ones—and cook them in just enough water to cover them, with salt and a pinch of nutmeg and a piece of lemon peel, for twenty minutes after the water has boiled, starting from cold. I drain them (and keep the *cuisson*, of course, for some other purpose) and return them to their warm saucepan, which I cover with a thick cloth and stand in a warm corner of the stove for half an hour to let the steam evaporate into the cloth. Then I mash the potatoes in the pan with a strong fork, very carefully and thoroughly until I know that there are no lumps, and then I work in butter, in bits—a quarter of a pound for three pounds of potatoes. When the butter has been well worked in, I add, gradually, enough milk to make a soft *purée* that slowly slips off the fork when I hold it up. Finally, I sprinkle in a little lemon juice and some white pepper, and beat the *purée* with a wire whisk. I then put it while still hot into a colander lined with thickly buttered greaseproof paper. When I want to reheat it, I stand the colander over a pot of water that barely simmers, and cover it with a lid.

Vegetables

CREAMED SPINACH

I am particularly fond of spinach, but the first time that I cooked it, following the instructions in my earliest (English) cookery book, I decided never to do it again because it took several hours. Six pounds of it (for six people) quite filled the kitchen sink, and the business of removing the stalk and the mid-rib from every one of all those leaves took the whole morning; and later there was the endless process of pushing it all through a fine sieve. I now realize that all that toil was simply a waste of time. I leave the stalks and mid-ribs alone, and never sieve my spinach because I find that it is much nicer when just chopped.

I wash the leaves in two lots of water, to get rid of mud and grit; and while it is floating in the water I pick out the yellowish leaves, and the odd bits of grass and chickweed. Then I put it all in a huge heap on the draining-board and press it down as hard as I can to expel the water, turning it over and pressing it several times. Then I chop it up roughly but quite thoroughly with a large sharp knife. (And all this takes only a few minutes.) Then I cram it into the biggest saucepan, and if it won't all go in, I use the fish-kettle or the preserving pan, instead. I put in no water, because the leaves are still pretty wet; I sprinkle some salt over it and cook gently for about half an hour, stirring frequently and adding more salt from time to time. Then I drain it well through a colander, pressing it down hard to extract all the liquid that will come out of it (and that makes excellent soup.) Then I put the spinach back into the saucepan, and set it over low heat and stir into it four ounces of butter for six pounds of spinach, sprinkling it with pepper occasionally, until the butter is dissolved among the mass of leaves. Then I sprinkle in gradually three good spoonfuls of flour, stirring vigorously all the time, until the spinach is no longer at all sloppy but looks as if it had been dressed with cream. I reheat it in a colander lined with greaseproof buttered paper, over simmering water, with a lid over it.

Vegetables

CREAMED CABBAGE, KALE, OR SPRING GREENS

I cook this in just the same way as in the last recipe, but chop more finely. This dish is the eye-opener of all time for those who only the wet English cabbage know.

BRUSSELS SPROUTS

In the nursery I was vainly incited to eat these hellish little vegetables, so smelly and watery, by being told that they were Fairy Cabbages. I have grown to like them, but only when they are cooked according to the best principles, with a pinch of bicarbonate of soda and a squeeze of lemon juice, in boiling salted water, and then most thoroughly drained on a sieve; and even then I must have them dressed with a cheese sauce. I make this with half a pint of Béchamel sauce, and stir into it two spoonfuls of grated cheese and a pinch of nutmeg and a pinch of caraway seeds. When cooking ahead, I leave the sprouts to drain (head downwards on the sieve) and leave the sauce covered with wet greaseproof paper. About forty minutes before it is to be served, I butter a pie dish and put the sprouts into it and pour the stirred sauce over them, and put it into a low oven (320 deg., Gas, No. 2). When taken out, the sauce ought to be bubbling. This is a vegetable dish that ought really to be eaten by itself, but it goes well with casserole of pigeon and especially with any *réchauffé* of chicken.

LEEKS

Leeks are excellent creatures, but a nuisance to clean, unless they have been grown in paper collars to keep the earth out of their folds. I find that the best way to clean them is to cut them into three-inch lengths, and to rinse each one under the cold tap, unfolding them as this is done and then wrapping them up again. I cook them in boiling salted water with a squeeze of lemon juice, and drain them propped up on end round the sides of a sieve to let all the water drip out, for they must never be served sodden

Vegetables

(but are, only too often). I reheat them, still up-ended, in an unlined colander over simmering water, for not more than half an hour; and dish them up with a Béchamel sauce which has been flavoured with lemon juice and paprika.

BROAD BEANS

These are among the most delicious of our vegetables, while they are still young. If they are allowed to become large and leathery and tough, they lose their charm, as people do. I cook young broad beans in boiling salted water until they are tender, drain them well, and dress them with a little butter and a dusting of pepper. They need no sauce, and can be reheated in their dish set over gentle steam with a pat of butter on top of them, and the lid on the dish. The result is wonderfully different from the wrinkled brown objects stuck together with flour-and-water paste which are sometimes slapped down on one's plate in horrible hotels.

I never throw away the pods of young broad beans, but cook them as a separate vegetable. (In this respect only I humbly venture to differ from the *pronunciamenti* of M. André Simon, who says that they are inedible.) I remove the strings at the sides, cut the pods into short pieces, and cook them in the same way that I cook the beans. They can be mixed with the beans to make a bigger dish of vegetables, and cooked together, so that two pounds of really young broad beans will do for six people if the pods are used too. Plenty of butter should be added.

Cold young broad beans are excellent in salads, either raw or cooked. The *cuisson* makes the foundation for good soups and sauces, but has the visual disadvantage of being black, and must therefore be coloured with tomatoes or saffron, or used with a brown stock.

PEAS

Peas, too, must be really young. Old, floury ones taste of nothing, and have a disagreeable texture. Early peas are the really perfect summer vegetable, but the strong-skinned late marrowfats

Vegetables

beloved of the English caterer are not, in my opinion, worth cooking. I cook young peas with a sprig of mint in boiling salted water with a spoonful of sugar, drain them well, and reheat them in a colander lined with buttered greaseproof paper, with a pat of butter on top of them, and a lid over them, above a pot of simmering water.

YOUNG CARROTS AND TURNIPS

Very young root vegetables are quite delicious, but too often in our Islands they are left to swell in the ground until they are large and tough and fit only to flavour stews. I extract mine—either from garden or greengrocer—when the carrots are no bigger than my finger, and the turnips not larger than a golf-ball. I cook them in salted water, starting from cold, until they are tender, drain them, and mix them with butter and chopped parsley while they are still hot, so that they are well oiled. They are reheated in a covered dish over simmering water in a pan beneath, with a spoonful of brown sugar and a sprinkling of lemon juice on top of them.

CREAMED PARSNIPS

This good vegetable is loathed by most English people, though not by the Irish, who here show their gastronomic good sense. In England I never have a dish of parsnips unless I know that my guests will not with one accord refuse it, but in Ireland I never think twice about it. I cook peeled, cut-up parsnips in salted water with a squeeze of lemon juice until they are tender—starting from cold—and then drain them, and mash them well with a fork with pepper, nutmeg, a few bits of butter, and a little cream. Then I return them to the warm saucepan and cook them for a few minutes longer, stirring until the *purée* is thick. It is reheated over simmering water in a colander lined with buttered greaseproof paper, with a lid over it.

SAUTÉ PARSNIPS

I cut up peeled parsnips into small cubes, and shake them in

Vegetables

seasoned flour before I toss them in hot oil until they are golden all over and beginning to brown. Then they are drained on crumpled paper, sprinkled well with salt and pepper, and put into a buttered shallow dish. They are reheated in this, uncovered, in a low oven for half an hour.

MIXED ROOTS

This is a good solid dish of vegetables with a strong flavour and it does well with mild-tasting food such as chicken or guinea-fowl. I prepare and cook equal quantities of turnips, carrots, parsnips, and celeriac, and drain them thoroughly for some time when they are done. Then I chop them into small cubes. I make a horse-radish sauce by stirring a small grated horse-radish and the juice of half a lemon into half a pint of Béchamel sauce and mixing it well, with a pinch of mixed spice. The vegetables and sauce are stirred together while the sauce is warm, with a good spoonful of chopped parsley. The whole thing is heated in a covered dish over simmering water.

Vegetables cooked according to all these recipes are suitable for eating with meat or birds, when a vegetable is wanted as an accompaniment. The recipes which follow, however, are for vegetable dishes intended to be served as a separate course, and I really do think it would be a great mistake to mix any of them up on a plate with anything else.

Vegetables as a Separate Course

SPINACH WITH CREAM CHEESE

The spinach is prepared as in the recipe for Creamed Spinach (see p. 123) until it has been cooked, drained, and returned to the saucepan. Then, instead of using butter, I stir into it the same quantity of soft cream cheese, or home-made curds, and some nutmeg as well as pepper; and when it is well stirred and the cheese melted into the spinach, a smaller quantity of flour is used to thicken the mixture, as the cream cheese is, and remains,

Vegetables

thicker than butter. It is put into a buttered ovenproof dish, covered with fresh bread-crumbs and little bits of butter, and reheated in a moderate oven (350 deg., Gas, No. 3½) until the crumbs are browned.

PEAS WITH ONION

I put four ounces of fat bacon, cut up, into a saucepan over low heat, and when the fat comes out freely I put in two chopped shallots, and shake and stir until the shallots are melted and just beginning to colour. Then I put in a quart of young shelled peas, with a teacupful of hot water, salt and pepper and a pinch of mixed herbs, and several bits of butter. They are stirred gently until the butter is melted, then I sprinkle in a spoonful of flour and go on stirring until the peas are cooked. This dish ought not to be reheated, but if it is made half an hour or so before it is to be eaten, it can be kept warm successfully in a double saucepan over hot water. It can be made with tinned peas, well drained— the small ones, not the starchy, tasteless, marrowfat kind.

FRENCH BEANS WITH CHEESE

Having removed the strings and sliced the beans slantwise (but very young ones need not be sliced) I cook them in boiling salted water with a pinch of bicarbonate of soda, with the lid off, and let them boil fast. When they are tender, I drain them, and put them in a colander and immediately mix with them some very fresh soft Cheddar or Cheshire cheese cut up in little slivers. I sprinkle them with pepper, and mix the cheese well among the warm beans. They are reheated in the colander over simmering water for half an hour or forty minutes. The heat softens the cheese and disseminates its flavour among the beans, but the pieces remain not quite melted, and the result is delicious.

MUSHROOMS FELIX

I break up a pound of mushrooms into smallish pieces, and

Vegetables

chop the stalks finely. They are cooked very slowly in a double saucepan, with two spoonfuls of bacon fat and two of veal broth, with salt and pepper. When they are soft, they are drained well, put into a buttered fireproof dish which has a lid, and sprinkled with chopped parsley. The *cuisson* is made up to almost a pint by the addition of tomato soup (see p. 32). I make a large white *roux* with two spoonfuls of butter and two of flour, stir the liquid into it, and add the juice of one lemon. This sauce is stirred until it is pretty thick, and then poured over the mushrooms, and the dish is covered at once with wet greaseproof paper. It is reheated, with the lid over the paper, for half an hour or forty minutes in a low oven (320 deg., Gas, No. 2). This dish is enough for eight people. Freshly made thin brown toast is an agreeable accompaniment to it.

GLOBE ARTICHOKES OILED

I get as many artichokes as there are people to feed, unless I can get really small, young ones which are far the best, and in that case I have two for each person. I cut off the stalks and snip off the spikes of the leaves, and then force them open and scoop out the 'choke' with a teaspoon. I mix some good oil with salt and pepper, stir it well, and put half a spoonful of it into the heart of each artichoke. Then I arrange them in a pan so that they are all upright, supported by each other in the pan which is just large enough to contain them. I pour cold salted water into the pan until it comes a little more than half-way up the artichokes, put the lid on, and bring the water slowly to the boil, and simmer for half an hour. The artichokes are then taken out and put on a sieve, still upright, so that they do not lose all of the unctuous stuff in their hearts, but the water drains from their leaves. The *cuisson* is then measured, and made into a thick sauce with the appropriate quantity of white *roux*, being cooked with a crushed clove of garlic and flavoured with lemon juice and pepper, and as much more salt as is needed. The clove is removed when it is finished, and the saucepan is covered at once with wet greaseproof paper. The artichokes are reheated in a colander over steaming water for half an hour (still upright) and transferred (upright) to a hot dish,

Vegetables

and the sauce, which has been reheated and stirred in its double saucepan over hot water, is put into a warmed sauce-boat.

These artichokes are just as good as a cold dish, put into a china serving-platter when they are drained, and the sauce chilled in the refrigerator.

AUBERGINES, 'PEPPERS' AND TOMATOES

For eight people, I buy four aubergines (madly called egg plants in England), four pimentos, either green, yellow, or red, and a pound of tomatoes. I wash, dry, and slice the aubergines; wash, dry, and slice the pimentos, and remove their seeds; and scald, skin, seed and chop the tomatoes. I put two spoonfuls of oil into a thick pan, and when it is hot I put in the aubergines, and stir until they begin to melt over low heat. Then I put in the pimentos, and go on stirring, and when the mass begins to solidify, I put in the tomatoes, and season it all with plenty of salt and pepper, and go on stirring until the whole thing is cooked and consolidated. It is reheated in a colander lined with buttered greaseproof paper over hot water, turned into a hot dish, and served with thin slices of buttered pumpernickel.

STUFFED PIMENTOS (HOT)

I choose large well-shaped peppers, either green, yellow, or red, one for two people. I simmer them in salted water for twenty minutes, and then cut them in half and turn the halves upside-down to drain. When they are quite drained, I scoop out the seeds and the ribs—and it is important to remove every seed, because even one will scorch the tongue of any guest who has not spent a lifetime living on outrageous curries. I stuff them with barley which has been cooked with vegetables (see p. 112), which I first mix well with an equal quantity of parsnip sauce (see p. 29) which must be really thick, and I stir chopped parsley into this mixture before filling the peppers with it. They are reheated in a covered dish in the oven, with a few spoonfuls of any kind of stock in the dish, for half an hour or forty minutes in low heat (320 deg., Gas, No. 2), then transferred to another dish without the liquid.

Vegetables

STUFFED PIMENTOS (COLD)

I cook the pimentos in the same way, and then stuff them with a mixture of cream cheese, finely chopped garlic sausage and gherkins, and cooked, chopped mushrooms. I sprinkle some caraway seeds, salt and pepper, and a little lemon juice into this stuffing as I pound it all together with a wooden spoon. It is crammed firmly into the halved peppers, which must be quite cold before being stuffed. I then chop finely a spoonful of black olives, whip a little cream which I flavour with lemon juice, and whisk the chopped olives into it. Each pepper is covered with a neat topping of this cream, and they are put in the refrigerator until they are wanted.

ASPARAGUS

Asparagus is cooked in simmering salted water for twenty minutes if it is the thick, white kind, or for about seventeen minutes if it is the thin, green kind—more delicious, in my opinion. It is then carefully drained without damage to the delicately attached heads. (I cook mine in the fish-kettle, and lift it out on the drainer, which simplifies the operation.) It is not very easy to reheat cooked asparagus, but I have evolved a way of doing it which is tolerably satisfactory. I lay the well-drained asparagus on a sheet of thickly buttered greaseproof paper, wrap the paper lightly round it so that it is quite enclosed in a loose parcel, and put this parcel on a cake rack over a baking tin full of hot water in a moderate oven for about twenty minutes. Then the asparagus is slid gently out of the paper on to a hot, flat dish. This method makes it taste as if it had only just been cooked, but has the disadvantage of making the stalks buttery to hold. *Hollandaise* sauce, kept hot in a double saucepan, accompanies it if it is the thick, white asparagus, and if the green kind, melted butter that is foaming hot. If I have either kind of asparagus cold, I always make a *hollandaise* sauce for it, cold too (but not chilled, as some restaurants produce it. There is no satisfaction to be got out of dipping asparagus heads into an icy sauce, and no flavour either).

Salads

I make only two kinds of salad dressing, a plain one and a cream one, but sometimes I dress a rather solid salad with mayonnaise sauce.

PLAIN SALAD DRESSING

I put a clove of garlic and a slice of raw shallot into a small bowl, and crush them firmly, with salt, pepper, half a spoonful of sugar, and the juice of half a lemon, and then stir until the sugar is dissolved. I then add two spoonfuls of olive oil (I think good Lucca oil is the best), and stir vigorously, and strain this dressing into a *large* bowl or dish, so that there is plenty of room for stirring the salad about until it is all quite coated with the dressing and there is no residue in the bottom of the dish. (I think it is important that salad should be loosely served in an ample container. I recollect ridiculous bowls of lettuce crammed in tightly, and absurdly decorated with a pattern of tomato and hard-boiled egg on the top, prepared by people who were concerned with presenting a decorative dish and not with its gastronomic qualities and the convenience of their guests. One should be able to dip into a bowl of salad, without fear of pushing over its rim the contents of a brimming little bowl.)

This dressing may be made in larger quantities, and kept in a cool place for several days.

Salads

CREAM SALAD DRESSING

I make this in the same way that I make the plain dressing, except that I use cream instead of oil, mixed with a small teaspoonful of made mustard. This dressing does not keep well in warm weather.

WINTER HARD SALAD

I make a cream dressing, and put it into a large bowl. I peel, cut up, and core a pound of hard dessert apples, and put them into the bowl as I cut them up, and stir them so that they are coated with the dressing before they can turn brown. I then separate, wash, and wipe a head of celery, discard the green part, and chop the rest small and stir it into the dressing. Finally I peel and cut into cubes two large cold boiled beetroots and put them into the bowl, sprinkle chopped parsley over it all, and mix it all thoroughly. It is a beautiful pink colour.

SALAD OF PEARS AND CUCUMBER

I peel a small cucumber, and cut it into large dice, then peel two large pears which are only just ripe, and cut them into cubes; and then I peel, and chop small, one shallot. I chop up the heart of a young cabbage, and a handful of parsley, and mix it all together with cream dressing. This salad is good with duck, goose, and game.

HEART OF LETTUCE SALAD

For four people, I choose a large firm-hearted cabbage lettuce and remove the outer leaves. I wash the heart under the cold tap and drain it well, and then divide it into four pieces, which I put on a flat dish. I wash and chop small a small, seeded pimento (a red or yellow one, for choice) and scatter the pieces over the quarters of lettuce. Then I pour plenty of plain dressing over each quarter, so that it soaks down into it.

Salads

CORN SALAD WITH WHITE ENDIVE

Corn salad is a delicious green salad plant which used to be called Lamb's Lettuce. It is not easy to buy, unfortunately, although it is always available in America, and I have a Scottish gardening book published in 1831 which lists it as a regular necessity in the kitchen garden. I wish that gardeners would produce more of it, and greengrocers demand it. It grows in small bunchy heads of green leaves, and the roots must be cut off and the heads washed and dried and separated. For a large handful of corn salad, I slice one head of white Dutch endive, mix it with the corn-salad leaves, and dress it with cream dressing.

NEW YEAR SALAD

I hard-boil four eggs, and blanch and peel four tomatoes, and put them in the refrigerator to chill, which makes them easier to slice. I slice finely the white parts of two heads of celery, and four white Dutch endives, and then slice thinly the chilled eggs and tomatoes. I wash, seed, and slice finely one pimento—or, if they are out of season, I use a tinned one, carefully drained. I arrange all these sliced vegetables on a flat dish, and pour plenty of cream dressing over them, and sprinkle finely chopped chervil or lemon balm on the top—or parsley if I cannot get the herbs.

The big oval entrée dishes of a dinner service do very well for these salads that must be served in flat dishes instead of in bowls.

COS LETTUCE SALAD

I put the unbroken leaves of a big, crisp cos lettuce into a wide deep dish with a lot of chives chopped small. (I use spring onions, chopped, if chives are out of season.) I dress the salad with plain dressing, making sure that every leaf is well coated and finally cast a light sprinkling of sugar over it, just before it is served.

Salads

HEART OF CABBAGE SALAD

I chop up the heart of a firm white cabbage, and mix it with plenty of chopped chives or spring onions, and chopped parsley, and a handful of cooked sultanas which have been well drained. I dress it with cream dressing, and finally give it a light sprinkling of red pepper, which somewhat disguises the inescapable fact that raw cabbage does taste like the smell of india-rubber hot-water bottles.

BALLYMORE SALAD

I wash and dry a lot of young nasturtium leaves and mix them with whole small lettuce leaves—the thinnings of either cos or round lettuce—and chopped spring onions, and dress the salad with plain dressing.

GARDEN SALAD

I make this salad with a little of everything that I can find in the kitchen garden. Young broad beans and peas (raw), dandelion leaves, nasturtium leaves, thinnings of lettuce and spinach, a baby marrow or two, little carrots, spring onions and chives, a few radishes, some sprigs of sage and mint and other herbs, plenty of parsley, and a few cold cooked waxy potatoes will make a fine diversified salad, which can be extended with tomatoes, hard-boiled eggs, cucumber, chopped cabbage heart, and anything else available. I grate the carrot, chop the herbs, slice the solid things, and wash and dry the green-stuff. It is all mixed together with a plain dressing in a really big bowl. (I use a soup tureen, which affords plenty of room for mixing, and for delving in for tidbits.)

CUCUMBER AND EGG AND APPLE SALAD

I slice a peeled cucumber, three peeled small dessert apples, and three hard-boiled eggs, and arrange them on a shallow dish

Salads

and cover them at once with plenty of cream dressing, then sprinkle them with chopped chives, or spring onions, and parsley. This is a good salad to have with cold ham.

WATERCRESS AND TOMATO SALAD

I arrange whole, skinned tomatoes in a dish with sprigs of watercress, and dress them with a plain dressing and chopped chives or spring onions scattered on top.

Puddings

My repertoire of puddings is limited by the fact that I don't like hot ones much, and really prefer cold fruit and cream (or ice-cream) to the most cunning confections. So my puddings tend to be simple ones, but I sometimes make an elaborate one for people who particularly like this sort of food, especially for parties at Christmas-time. More often than not, however, the pudding at my dinner-parties consists of a bowl of fruit with ice and cream.

FRESH FRUIT WITH ICE AND CREAM

I buy a block of vanilla ice-cream, of the size curiously called a Family Brick and put it in the refrigerator. I prepare ripe fresh fruit in the summer, such as strawberries, raspberries, loganberries, black currants, apricots, or blackberries, half-fill a china bowl with them, and put it in a cold place. In the winter I sometimes make a fresh-fruit salad, with ripe pears, apples, bananas, peeled grapes and mandarin oranges, instead; or I buy deep-frozen raspberries or loganberries (but not strawberries, they are too juicy when thawed). An hour before pudding-time I unpack the Family Brick and put it on top of the fruit in the bowl, and leave it in the larder; and I whip plenty of cream and leave it ready. Just before it is served, the ice-cream and fruit are stirred together, and the whipped cream put on top of them.

Puddings

APPLE AND DAMSON MERINGUE

I use a small tin of damsons, and drain them over a saucepan until all the syrup is in the pan. Then I cook in this syrup two pounds of apples, peeled and cut up, until they are soft, with two spoonfuls of sugar, two ounces of butter, and the juice of half a lemon. (More sugar will be needed if the apples are not fairly sweet ones.) This *purée* is pressed through a wire sieve, with the damsons, and well stirred with a dash of maraschino, then the yolks of two eggs, beaten, are stirred into it, the mixture is put into a double saucepan over simmering water and stirred until it is thick. It is then turned into an ovenproof dish to cool. When it is cold, I beat the whites of four eggs stiffly, and gradually whisk into them four ounces of icing sugar. This meringue is spread over the cold *purée*, and cooked in a very cool oven (280 deg., Gas, No. 1) until it has set and just begun to colour. The pudding is served chilled.

DIPLOMATE

For this pudding I buy a small tin of apricots, and half a pound of small sponge finger biscuits, and if they are not really thin fingers, I split them. I drain the juice from the apricots into a saucepan, and cook in it two pounds of apples, peeled and cut up, with two ounces of butter and two spoonfuls of sugar, and when they are soft I press them through a wire sieve into a bowl. I dissolve enough gelatine to set a pint of liquid, in very little water, and, when it is perfectly dissolved I strain it into the apple *purée*, add a spoonful of brandy, and stir it well. I butter a pie dish (a fairly deep one makes the best mould for a Diplomate, I find—round moulds produce circular puddings which have to be turned out on to serving-dishes of enormous diameter). I spread a half-inch layer of the *purée* in the pie dish, cover it with a layer of sponge fingers, chop the drained apricots small and spread them over the sponge fingers. Another layer of *purée* covers them, then a layer of sponge fingers, and the rest of the *purée*, which

Puddings

must fill the dish brim-full. (If there is not quite enough *purée* to fill it, I make a little more with a spoonful of apricot jam melted in a little hot water and a couple of apples cooked in it with a little sugar and a bit of butter; and stir into it a little dissolved gelatine, and a teaspoonful of brandy.) The brimming pie dish is covered with a layer of buttered greaseproof paper, and then with something hard and flat, such as the chopping-board or the lid of a big saucepan, and weights are put on it. This is to make the mixture consolidate as it cools, for the swelling sponge fingers would push up the top surface if it were not weighted down, whereas they are expected to swell sideways and make the Diplomate compact. The next day, I take off the weights and the lid and put the dish in the refrigerator. I whip half a pint of cream with a teaspoonful of icing sugar and a teaspoonful of brandy until it is stiff. Finally I unmould the Diplomate by sliding a knife round the sides of the dish, reversing it on to a large oval serving-dish, and giving it a smart tap on the bottom. The Diplomate emerges firm and shapely, and I cover it with the stiffly whipped cream, and put it back into the refrigerator until it is wanted. It is enough for eight.

CRÈME D'AGRUMES

First I beat four eggs together lightly, and put them in a double saucepan over water that is only just simmering. I stir into them a cup of orange juice and half a cup of lemon juice, and four ounces of sieved icing sugar, and go on stirring until the mixture thickens to the consistency of thin cream. I then pour it into a bowl, and when it is cool, put it into the refrigerator to chill. Then I prepare eight very ripe small Tangerine oranges—or Mandarines or Clementines—removing all the white part carefully, and extracting the pips with a skewer through the smallest possible hole in each section. I then cut up four Canary bananas (which have a far better flavour than the big ones) and mix them with the sections of orange. Then I whip half a pint of cream with a teaspoonful of icing sugar and a teaspoonful of maraschino, and when it is stiff I fold it into the orange-lemon cream which has been thoroughly

Puddings

chilled. The fruit is then mixed with this, carefully, and the mixture is put either into a serving-dish or into separate glasses, and the surface sprinkled with chopped blanched almonds.

ZABAGLIONE

A third of a pint of white wine, two spoonfuls of Marsala, and three spoonfuls of sugar are brought slowly to the boil. Meanwhile I put a large deep pudding basin in the oven to get really hot, or else fill it with boiling water—a merely warm basin won't do. Then I separate the yolks of four eggs from the whites, and have the yolks at hand on the table, with the egg-beater beside them. As soon as the liquid is at the boiling point, I put the egg-yolks into the very hot basin and beat them fast with the egg-beater for about ten seconds; then, still beating, I pour in the boiling wine fairly fast, and go on beating for about another minute, or a little longer. Then I pour the mixture into six strong, shallow, thick wineglasses that are standing ready on the table. After about three minutes it will have set, and can be served. However, there is never anyone in my kitchen who can carry out this operation while the previous course is being eaten in the dining-room, and I certainly won't go and do it myself in the middle of dinner, and so I make the Zabaglione an hour beforehand and leave it in a cold place to chill, as it is equally delicious when eaten cold. (This is a dish which must inevitably be presented in what the M.O.F. used coyly to call 'individual servings'.)

CHOCOLATE MOUSSE

For each person, one egg and one ounce of plain chocolate are needed—I use Menier, but any other good slab chocolate will do. The chocolate is melted in a large bowl over gentle heat until it is soft, then the bowl is removed from the heat and the yolks of the eggs are stirred into it until it is well mixed. The whites of the eggs are beaten until they are very stiff, and stirred into the contents of the bowl, and the mixture is turned into a dish, or into separate small pots. It should be left in a cold place for at least twelve hours.

Puddings

PEARS WITH CHOCOLATE SAUCE

I get large stewing pears for this dish, and peel them, cut them in half, remove the cores, and stew them very slowly in water with some sugar and a little red wine until they are cooked but not very soft. The water is drained off and made up to half a pint, if necessary, with water, to make enough sauce for six pears. The pears are drained, cooled, and put into the refrigerator to chill. The liquid is heated with a spoonful of butter, half a spoonful of maraschino, and four ounces of cocoa, and stirred carefully, with the addition of as much sugar as it needs, until it is quite smooth. Then I mix a teaspoonful of cornflour with a little water to a cream, stir it into the sauce, and reduce the sauce by boiling it fairly fast until it is quite thick. It is covered, when finished, with wet greaseproof paper, and reheated in a double saucepan just before serving, stirred well, and poured over the cold pears which are ready on a cold serving-dish.

CHOCOLATE AND APPLE PUDDING

Two pounds of apples, peeled and cored, are cut into pieces about as big as lumps of sugar, and simmered extremely gently in water with sugar and a piece of lemon peel until they are only just cooked but not really soft. I drain them over a saucepan until all the liquid has dripped into the saucepan, and add some port to the liquid to make it up to a pint. I stir into it two spoonfuls of butter and four ounces of cocoa, and more sugar, bearing in mind that cold sweet sauces need more sugar than hot ones. Two teaspoonfuls of cornflour are mixed with a little water to a smooth cream and stirred into the sauce when it is well blended, and the sauce is boiled fairly fast until it thickens, being stirred all the time. When it is really thick it is left to cool, covered with wet greaseproof paper. When it is quite cold the pieces of apple are gently mixed with it and it is put into a china bowl and chilled in the refrigerator. Finally it is covered with whipped cream.

Puddings

CHESTNUT CREAM

I blanch two pounds of chestnuts after slitting the shells, then shell them and skin them, and cook them in boiling water with a piece of lemon peel until they are soft enough. I put them through the mincer, put half of the *purée* aside to cool, and work into the other half two ounces of butter and a spoonful of rum until it is a thick smooth paste. This is then spread in a layer on a flat serving-dish. I whip half a pint of cream, with a teaspoonful of icing sugar and a squeeze of lemon juice, until it is stiff, then fold it into the chilled remainder of the chestnut *purée*, and pile this on the layer in the dish. It is served very cold.

GOOSEBERRY SNOW

I cook a pound of ripe (or bottled) gooseberries with two spoonfuls of port and plenty of sugar and just enough water to prevent them sticking to the pan as they cook. They are pressed through a fine sieve. I then take from a pint of milk enough to mix two ounces of cornflour to a smooth paste. The rest of the milk is brought to the boil with two ounces of butter, and when the butter has quite melted into it, it is poured gradually on to the mixed cornflour, stirred thoroughly, and returned to the pan and stirred until it begins to thicken. Then I put in two ounces of sugar and a spoonful of lemon juice, and stir and cook until it is really thick. When nearly cold, the gooseberry *purée* is stirred into it, it is put into a china bowl, and chilled in the refrigerator. It is served covered with whipped cream.

COLD MOUSSE OF PRUNES

I soak a pound of prunes overnight in a pint of cold China tea. The next day I put in three ounces of sugar and a piece of lemon rind, and cook them gently until they are soft. They are then pressed through a fine sieve (minus the stones and the lemon peel) and I dissolve a pint-sized packet of powdered gelatine (or

Puddings

four leaves) in a glass of red wine, and strain this into the warm *purée* and stir it well. When it is cold, I fold into it half a pint of whipped cream, and chill it in the refrigerator before it is served.

BLACK CURRANT MOUSSE

I make this in exactly the same way, except that instead of prunes I use fresh black currants cooked in water, and rather more sugar.

RED CURRANT AND RASPBERRY JELLY

I make this in the summer, with fresh raspberries. A pound of raspberries is topped and put to chill in the refrigerator. I dissolve a pint-sized packet of powdered gelatine (or four leaves) in a cup of water, and strain it into a double saucepan with a cup of red wine and a one-pound pot of red currant jelly, and stir gently until it is all warm and well blended, adding sugar as I think necessary. I pour some of this jelly into a wetted mould, and when it has set, put a layer of raspberries on it. Meanwhile the jelly in the saucepan is stood over hot water until the jelly is just—but only just—melted enough to slide some out with a spoon, to cover the raspberries. This layer is then left to set, more raspberries are put on it, and the process is repeated until all the raspberries and jelly have been put in. The mould is chilled in the refrigerator until it is very firm, then unmoulded on to a serving-dish, and the jelly is covered with whipped cream.

PLUM PUDDING

I make my plum puddings in the winter, but I always keep them for a year, and sometimes for two years. (One was once left on a shelf in a cold larder and overlooked for three years, and proved to be excellent.) But of course they have to be kept in a cold, airy place. A cupboard in the kitchen won't do.

I use the biggest possible basin for mixing the pudding—a pre-

Puddings

serving pan, or an old-fashioned china wash-hand-stand basin, if there isn't a big enough kitchen bowl. The tedious toil of stirring is far worse if the mixture keeps on falling out because the bowl is too full to stir easily.

These are my ingredients: one pound each of raisins, currants, suet, and fresh bread-crumbs; half a pound each of sultanas and demerara sugar; a quarter of a pound each of ground almonds and golden syrup; three-quarters of a pound of mixed peel; ten eggs; a pint of milk; a gill of brandy; and a large pinch each of salt, nutmeg, and cinnamon.

I wash the fruit, pick off the stalks, and let it all dry well on the top of sieves in the warm kitchen all night. I stir up the milk and brandy in a jug with the eggs until they are well mixed together, but not beaten. I chop the suet small (but if I use prepared suet in a packet, I use only three-quarters of a pound of bread-crumbs, because the suet is coated with flour). I mix the fruit, suet, bread-crumbs, sugar, peel, and seasoning well in the basin, warm the syrup and stir it in, and then add gradually the contents of the jug, and stir, and go on stirring. Of course I get everyone else in the house to stir it, for luck, and if there are several energetic people this is a great help, because undoubtedly plum pudding does need a lot of stirring. Only by really complete mixing can the best, richest, darkest pudding be achieved. When I feel sure that it has been stirred enough, I butter the pudding basins—one very large and two very small, or one fairly large and two medium-sized ones—and I use very fresh butter, not old butter-papers. I fill the basins right up to the top, pressing down the mixture firmly and evenly with the side of a cup, until the basins are quite full and the surface is flat. I put a buttered round of greaseproof paper over each basin, then an unbuttered one, and tie them on, and snip off the edges of the paper below the string. Then I put pudding-cloths over the paper, and get someone to put a finger on the knot when I tie them down with string, as I want to get the string as tight as possible. I take up the four corners of each cloth, and sew them together on top. Then I put the basins into saucepans, or into the preserving pan and the fish-kettle, with water up to within half an inch of their tops—and so, of course, if I boil

Puddings

two in one container, they are basins of the same size. The water is brought slowly to simmering point—not more, or it wets the tops too much—and kept simmering for twelve hours, being kept at this level by additions of hot water when necessary. (It may seem unnecessary to add that this cooking need not be done at one stretch, but I knew a woman who thought that it had to be, and so sat up with her puddings and spent a *nuit blanche* in the kitchen.) When the boiling is done, I wipe the basins and put them on the top shelf in the larder and forget them for a year.

To prepare the pudding on Christmas Day, I put the basin in a saucepan and boil it, in the same way, for four hours, then remove the cloth and the paper, and turn out the pudding into a hot dish —a strong, deep one, if it is to enter the dining-room *en flammes*. I have brandy butter with it, which I make by working two ounces of sugar and a spoonful of brandy into half a pound of butter until it is well mixed and no longer wet, and then chilling it in the refrigerator.

Slices of cold plum pudding, sprinkled with sugar and eaten with thick cream, make a really splendid cold pudding for Boxing Day. In my opinion, it should never, never be fried.

SHAM MINCE PIES

What I don't like about mince pies is the abundance of pie and the shortage of mincemeat. (When I do make this pudding, I make it large and flat and uncovered, like a treacle tart. But I hardly ever make it.) However, an excellent imitation mince pie can be produced at a moment's notice with no more effort than is involved in spreading mincemeat thickly on a cream-cracker biscuit and making it hot in the oven. These Christmas-time tidbits have all the advantages lacked by the real article—plenty of mincemeat, a crisp and not crumbly foundation, and no lid, and are eaten in one's fingers. Cream-cracker biscuits, piping hot, are really better than pastry as a conveyor of mincemeat. But no other biscuits will do.

Puddings

CURDS WITH SUGAR

I put a quart of milk into a jug and stand it in a warm place until it has 'turned'—this takes about twenty-four hours. The whey is then poured away, and the curds are put into a piece of muslin and suspended over a bowl in the larder until they no longer drip—and this takes another day. Then the solid lump of curd is worked with a few drops of lemon juice and plenty of demerara sugar and a pinch or two of caraway seeds with a wooden spoon in a large bowl, until these flavourings are well distributed through it. It is then put into a serving-dish and covered with stiffly whipped cream.

Menus for Dinner and Supper

I have chosen menus for a Dinner, a Special Dinner, and a Supper for each month of the year, with due regard to what is seasonable and plentiful. The dinners are designed to be dished-up and served without any assistance, and planned so that only one journey from dining-room to kitchen is necessary. The special dinners are the ones which I cook when I have engaged my invaluable Mrs. Morning-Help to return in the evening and dish-up for me, and bring the food to the dining-room when I ring for it. These may have more than one hot course, and include dishes to which a sauce or some other preparation has to be added at the last moment. The suppers are designed to be reheated quickly on returning from a concert or the play, and consist of only two courses, usually a hot one and a cold one.

For the special dinners I have suggested the wines which I think would be appropriate and agreeable without any great extravagance. (In this context I should like to point out that all these dinners are intended to end with dessert.)

I have made no suggestions as to what could be drunk with the dinners and suppers. Enterprising wine-lovers will have plenty of ideas of their own, other people will drink beer or cider or water (but not, I hope, bottled fruit juice). I do hope, however, that the beer-drinkers and the cider-drinkers will contrive to cool their bottles, either in the refrigerator, or by standing them for twenty-four hours in a basin of water with a wet cloth over them, the ends of the cloth soaking up the water and producing evaporation to cool the bottles.

Menus for Dinner and Supper

Cooking induces a sense of thankfulness, and so does writing about it. I end this book with the words of the old Grace before Meat: 'Bless all these good creatures to Thy use, and us to Thy Service.'

January Menus

DINNER
Le Paté de la Comtesse de Preux
*

Braised Oxtail
Mashed Potatoes
*

Apple and Damson Meringue

SPECIAL DINNER
Turbot in White Wine   Spanish Seco
*

Mousse of Turkey   Meursault 1953
Sauté Parsnips.   Corn Salad with Endive
*

Zabaglione

SUPPER
Tomato and Cheese Gnocchi
*

Sham Mince Pies

February Menus

DINNER
Brown Veal Soup
*

Braised Pork
Mashed Potatoes
Watercress and Tomato Salad
*

Chestnut Cream

Menus for Dinner and Supper

SPECIAL DINNER

Moules Béchamel   Pouilly Fuissé 1953

*

Burgundian Steak   Fleurie 1952
Green Salad

*

Mushrooms Felix

SUPPER

Cold Mousse of Veal   New Year Salad

*

Spaghetti with Tomatoes

March Menus

DINNER

Eggs on Ham in Aspic

*

Mderbel   Mashed Potatoes

*

Black Currant Mousse

SPECIAL DINNER

Sole with Sour Cream   Yugoslav Silvaner

*

Braised Fillet of Veal   Ch. La Lagune 1950
Mashed Potatoes   Leeks

*

Crème d'Agrumes   Ch. Coutet 1948

SUPPER

Baked Spanish Omelette

*

Curds with Sugar and Cream

Menus for Dinner and Supper

April Menus

DINNER
Coley au Bleu
*
Paté de Veau en Croûte
Corn Salad with Endive
*
Gnocchi

SPECIAL DINNER

Fillets of Plaice with Shallots	Blankenburg
*	(South Africa)
Steak with Mushrooms	Ch. La Lagune 1950
Mashed Potatoes Green Salad	
*	
Diplomate	Ch. Rabaud 1949

SUPPER
Cold Soft Eggs in Carrot Tops
*
Risotto with Prawns

May Menus

DINNER
Cold Soft Eggs in Green Mayonnaise
*
Fowl Stewed in Wine
New Potatoes   Watercress
*
Chocolate Mousse

Menus for Dinner and Supper

SPECIAL DINNER

Burgundian Eels	Beaujolais

*

Vol-au-Vent Latour	Moulin-à-Vent 1952
Salad of Cos Lettuce with Chives	

*

Asparagus with Hollandaise Sauce

SUPPER
Cold Baked Eggs

*

Hot Herrings in Oatmeal
Peas

June Menus

DINNER
Cold Fillets of Sole

*

Veal and Ham Soubise
New Potatoes   Lettuce Salad

*

Gooseberry Snow

SPECIAL DINNER

Gnocchi with Mushrooms and Bacon	Ch. Batailley 1950

*

Braised Fillet of Veal	Domaine de L'Eglise,
New Potatoes	Pomerol 1953

*

French Beans with Cheese

SUPPER
Shrimps in Aspic

*

Chicken Shepherd's Pie
Salad of Cucumber, Apple, and Egg

Menus for Dinner and Supper

July Menus

DINNER
Fillets of Fish in Aspic
*
Stuffed Fillet of Steak Braised
New Potatoes   Garden Salad
*
Strawberries with Cream and Ice-Cream

SPECIAL DINNER
Baked Fish Omelette   Entre-deux-Mers
*
Chicken Pie   Ch. Laujac 1952
Broad Beans
*
Peas with Onions

SUPPER
Cold Baked Stuffed Mackerel
Mayonnaise Sauce
*
Mouse of Veal
Ballymore Salad

August Menus

DINNER
Cold Chicken Soup
*
Goulasch of Veal
Mashed Potatoes
*
Raspberries in Red Currant Jelly

Menus for Dinner and Supper

SPECIAL DINNER
Halibut with Mushrooms and Bacon   Pouilly Fuissé

*

Bouchées Latour   Nuits St. Georges 1953
Lettuce Salad

*

Globe Artichokes (hot)

SUPPER
Hard Boiled Eggs with Tunny

*

Cold Risotto

September Menus

DINNER
Creamed Chicken Soup

*

Lamb Cutlets with Tomatoes and
Mushrooms
Mashed Potatoes

*

Cold Stuffed Peppers

SPECIAL DINNER
Tagliatelli Verdi   Beaujolais Rosé

*

Veal with Mushrooms   Chateauneuf du Pape
Heart-of-Lettuce Salad   1953

*

Aubergines, Peppers and Tomatoes

*

SUPPER
Soused Herrings

*

Hot Baked Eggs and Bacon

Menus for Dinner and Supper

October Menus

DINNER
Hare Soup
*

Couscous
*

Fresh Figs in Whipped Cream

SPECIAL DINNER
Baked Turbot   Sylvaner 1952
*

Mousse of Hare (hot)   Red Hermitage 1953
Creamed Spinach
*

Hot Stuffed Peppers

SUPPER
Gnocchi with Vegetables
Cold Pickled Pork with Prunes

November Menus

DINNER
Latvian Soup
*

Pigeons in Casserole
Mashed Potatoes   New Year's Salad
*

Chocolate Mousse

SPECIAL DINNER
Morocco Fillets of Fish   Muscadet
*

Casserole of Veal with Sherry   Ch. Palmer Margaux
Mashed Potatoes   Plain Green Salad   1950
*

Pears with Hot Chocolate Sauce Ch. Climens 1948

Menus for Dinner and Supper

SUPPER
Cold Pickled Pork Slices
Salad of Cucumber and Pears
*

Spinach with Cream Cheese

December Menus

DINNER
Haddock Soup
*

Ossi Bucchi   Risotto Milanese
*

Mousse of Prunes

SPECIAL DINNER
(Christmas Day)
Game Soup   Vin Rosé d'Anjou
*

Roast Turkey   Champagne Rosé
Roast Potatoes   Watercress
*

Plum Pudding   Brandy Butter

SUPPER
(for a large party)
Risotto Noël
Hard Winter Salad
*

Chocolate and Apple Pudding
and
Gooseberry Snow

DATE DUE

Demco, Inc. 38-293